Slackernomics

Slackernomics

◆

Basic Economics for People Who Think Economics is Boring

Dale Franks

iUniverse, Inc.
New York Lincoln Shanghai

Slackernomics
Basic Economics for People Who Think Economics is Boring

iUniverse, Inc.

For information address:
iUniverse, Inc.
2021 Pine Lake Road, Suite 100
Lincoln, NE 68512
www.iuniverse.com

ISBN: 0-595-31699-9 (pbk)
ISBN: 0-595-66379-6 (cloth)

Printed in the United States of America

For Chris, who believed

Contents

Acknowledgements

Special thanks for proofreading help go to Chris Johnson and Mike Riley, who did it even though they hate economics, and to Jon Henke for not only proofing the manuscript, but also offering valuable suggestions for its improvement. Nick Schulz, editor at TechCentralStation.com helped me more than he'll ever know. And he probably doesn't even know it.

All the mistakes, of course, are mine alone.

Introduction

I first started writing this book in 1996. At the time, I was hosting *The Business Day*, a daily financial news/interview radio program that was broadcast in Los Angeles on the unfortunately now-defunct Money Radio (KMNY AM-1600). The years I spent there were a far more valuable economic education than anything I received in college. Every day, I was privileged to speak with some of the finest economists in the world, including past and future Federal Reserve Governors, Nobel Laureates, presidential advisors and cabinet members, and the chief economists of some of the world's largest and best-known corporations. And, every day, I got to ask them pretty much whatever came into my mind.

It was the best learning experience of my life, and I even got paid for it. In the years since, of course, I've written and spoken on economics, politics, and foreign and military affairs. But nothing else I've done has equaled the exhilaration of talking live, on the air, to world class economic experts, asking them questions that interested me, and learning from their answers.

It was that learning experience that inspired me to begin writing this book.

A book on basic economics is hard to write. I should know, since I've been working on this one for eight years. If you're writing for people with an economic background, it's easier. They've already been through the schooling, replete with graphs, charts, math, statistics, and the rest. It's when you are starting from scratch and don't want to clutter up the pages with a lot of graphs and charts—and, as hard as I tried not to use them, there's still a few—that the challenge begins.

Oh, and making it interesting is a challenge, too. No one wants to read you droning on for page after page about moving the demand curve to the left, or any of that nonsense. That's really one of the reasons that so few people are interested in economics. Frankly, the general impression of economists is that they went into the field because they didn't quite have enough personality to be accountants.

That kind of perception makes economics a relatively unpopular field of study, and keeps a lot of otherwise intelligent, well-informed people from acquiring basic economic literacy. That's a problem.

We live in a society where domestic policy has a lot to do with economics. That's true whether you're talking about local bond issues for schools, or the federal budget. Every political issue that affects our daily lives has an economic component.

I'm writing this in an election year. The biggest domestic issues this year are all economic. Are we sending too many jobs overseas? Did the George W. Bush's tax cuts help or hurt the economy? How can we increase the number of new jobs?

Everyone in politics has an opinion, and no one is shy about sharing it. But, they can't all be right. The trouble is that you, as a voter, can't make a knowledgeable decision about who's right unless you know some of the basic principles behind the arguments that each side is making.

That's the purpose of this book.

Some things you learn might surprise you. John Maynard Keynes, probably *the* most influential economist of the 20th century, wrote that economists have the least influence on political issues where there is most agreement, and the most influence where there is the least agreement. So, it may surprise you to learn that there is nearly unanimous agreement among all economists, left or right, about certain issues.

For instance, the vast majority of economists believe that increasing the minimum wage leads to lower employment among the least skilled workers, usually the poor and minorities. Similarly, the vast majority of economists believe that free trade in goods and services—and, yes, employment—benefits everyone who engages in it. Economists believe that rent control reduces the available stock of housing, making it more difficult for people to find a place to live.

But, the fact that economists believe something, doesn't mean that, even if it's completely correct, our public policy should reflect it. Economics is a science. Because it deals with human beings and the choices they make, it isn't, like physics, a perfectly accurate one. Humans, after all, do a lot of strange stuff. Sometimes humans are pretty irrational.

Still, it's a science nonetheless, which means while it can tell us what will happen if we do certain things, it can't tell us whether we *should* do them. All it can do is to give us a fairly good idea about the costs and benefits of our decisions. Deciding whether we *want* to do something, after we have weighed the costs and benefits, is entirely up to us.

Usually the advocates for either side in a debate will give you the arguments that make their side sound better. It's up to you to cut through the hype they present, and figure out the truth.

What I hope to do in the pages that follow is to give you the information you need to make those decisions wisely. And, along the way, I hope not only to inform you, but entertain you.

My purpose is not to try to convince you of a particular viewpoint, but rather to give you information about what the broad consensus of opinion in the economic community actually is, so that you can form your own views.

Of course, we all have our biases, and I'm no different. I believe the free market produces the greatest amount of wealth for the greatest number of people. I believe that socialism has proven itself to be a catastrophic failure in every country where it's been tried. So, I obviously write from a free-market point of view.

Luckily, that puts me right in the mainstream of modern economic thought, too.

I hope you enjoy what follows.

Dale Franks
Escondido, CA
March, 2004

1

THE BIG PICTURE

THE BASICS

What is economics?

Economics has never been a widely respected science. In the 19th century, the British writer Thomas Carlyle called economics "pig philosophy" and the "dismal science". Since then, its reputation hasn't gotten much better.

The first real economist was a man named Adam Smith. In 1776, he published a book called *An Inquiry into the Nature and Causes of the Wealth of Nations*. In 1776, they didn't have catchy, cute titles like *Slackernomics*, so book titles tended to be a little too long and descriptive. In modern times, we just call Smith's book *The Wealth of Nations*.

The Wealth of Nations was the world's first explanation of economics. Indeed, Smith's definitions of wealth and labor are still used today.

It was also a truly revolutionary book. Not only did it explain almost everything known about economics at that time; it also opened up a whole new world of human behavior for study. From that one book, we have branched out into every type of economic study there is today.

And there are a lot of different types of economics. Below are just a few of the different study areas of economics. The explanations are very simple, but remember, some people spend their entire professional lives just studying one of these areas:

Microeconomics is the study of a single economic unit. It focuses on the behavior of a single business or industry, or even on the behavior of a single individual.

Macroeconomics is the study of the big picture. It studies the total amount of activity in the economy. It is especially concerned with economic growth, inflation, and unemployment.

Monetary Economics deals with how the government's activity affects the economy through the budget and taxation (fiscal policy), or by the central bank's regulation of the money supply (monetary policy.)

Agricultural Economics studies the farming system and the impact of farming policy on agriculture.

Labor Economics is the study the labor market, the effects of wages on prices, and the supply and demand for labor.

International Economics is the study of how nations trade with each other, how goods and currencies are exchanged.

There are many other areas of economics to study, each one a discipline that takes a lifetime to master.

But, what, precisely, are all these people studying?

In order to properly intimidate undergraduates, economics textbooks define economics as *the study of how humans respond to scarcity.*

That's the kind of econo-speak that causes potential economics students to skip right past the economics portion of the course catalog and go straight to Psych 101. Just reading it probably makes you start to nod off. Either that or you're asking yourself, "What does *that* mean?" In either case, you're probably thinking that it sounds like a pretty non-specific definition.

Really though, it isn't.

Every single resource you can think of, no matter how much of it we currently think we have, is finite. There's only so much beachfront property, for example. On the other hand, the number of people—well, men, actually—who want to have condos on the beach so that they can ogle bikini girls is practically unlimited. Compared to the number of people who want to live at the beach, property there is scarce.

Economics studies how people make choices when faced with the very real problem that everything is relatively scarce.

Now, that's a pretty broad ranging definition that can be applied to almost everything. If there are two kids and they want to split up a single candy bar, then deciding how to do it is an economic decision. Both kids want to be satisfied with their piece of the candy bar. Somehow, they have to decide what method to use to ensure that the candy bar is fairly rationed. Actually, if you're a parent of more than one child, you probably know that what both kids really want is the whole bar. But, since there's only one candy bar, it's a scarce resource compared to their desire. Somehow, they have to split it up in a way that provides the most satisfaction for both of them.

The economy is a candy bar writ large. There's only so many houses, so much oil, so many jobs. For any given length of time, only a finite number of goods can be produced, or services performed. Economics is the study of how society distributes all those things.

It might be neat to live in a world where everything you wanted could be had for the asking. In such a world, there wouldn't be any economics. Nothing would be scarce, so no one would have to make any decisions about how to use the scarce resources that are available.

Unfortunately, that's not the world we live in. In the real world, we are always faced with three basic questions:

1) What will we produce? At least half of the population, the women, will have no interest in building beachfront condos filled with bikini babes. They may be more interested in building something entirely different, like offices, and family homes.

2) How will resources be used in that production? We can use all sorts of mixes to reach the same result. For example, we can farm by hand, or we can use machinery. Farming by hand means that unemployment will be very, very low. It also means that fewer people will be

available to build houses, or program computers. The goal is to find a way to use resources in the most efficient way.

3) Who will consume the goods we produce? Every society faces this basic question, in which we have to balance equity with efficiency.

Wealth and Labor

Collectively, we refer to all those goods produced by a society as its wealth. Everything that is manufactured, every vegetable that is grown, every building that is built, and every suit coat that's hung up on a rack is a tiny bit of wealth.

Basically, wealth is all our stuff. America is considered a wealthy country economically because we make a lot of things. We don't just make the basic things we need, like food and shelter; we also make goods that are made simply to fulfill our desires. We don't need those extra goods, but we want them, anyway. So, in economic terms, rich societies are those that produce not only basic goods, but fun stuff, too.

Do you want to know how rich America is? We have so much wealth that we make padded toilet seats! We have so much wealth that we make stuff nobody in their right minds would want to buy. If you don't believe that, just watch one of the home shopping channels for a while.

On the other hand, poor countries are those that can't produce enough goods to keep everybody clothed, housed, and fed. In those countries, since basic needs can hardly be met, you don't find too much fun stuff. If there is not enough wealth to fulfill the people's basic needs, then there is no way for those non-essential desires to be fulfilled.

There's no home shopping channel in Bangladesh.

So, how is wealth produced? It's produced by labor. There are two kinds of labor, productive labor and non-productive labor.

Productive labor is the work that is actually involved in making physical goods, like washing machines or hamburgers. The autoworker in Flint, Michigan is involved in productive labor because the cars that roll off his assembly line are a part of the nation's production. The farmer in California's San Joaquin Valley is involved in productive labor, because his produce also counts as part of the nation's production of goods.

Labor that does not produce goods is called non-productive labor. There's nothing derogatory about the term non-productive. It just means that no goods are being produced as a result of that labor, so nothing is being added to the country's stock of physical items. But that doesn't mean that non-productive labor isn't necessary. A police officer is doing a necessary job. We need him to be on the beat every day. But his labor is non-productive. If you want to see another form of non-productive labor, go down to the DMV and watch the workers there. They're a prime example of non-productive labor.

Labor has to be paid in some way. After all, no one works for free. Most people have other interests they would rather pursue. So, they have to be paid in order to provide an incentive to do something other than stay home all day and watch Oprah.

Before the creation of money, most people worked at what is called subsistence farming. They grew just enough food to feed themselves and their families. They had to build their own homes and make their own clothes. People paid themselves, in effect, by producing their own food, clothing, and shelter.

If they wanted goods they couldn't make themselves, then they took some of their goods and traded them for things they wanted. For example, a farmer may have traded a bushel of wheat to a shoemaker in return for a pair of shoes. This was called a barter economy. The actual wealth of each person—the goods they produced—was used as a type of money.

But as economies got more and more complex, the barter system couldn't work. So, money was created as a medium of exchange. The actual goods were assigned a price, and money became a substitute for the actual goods.

Paying for labor by using money allows the economy to become larger and more complex. If the autoworker was paid by giving him the actual wealth he produced, his pay would consist of taking home a new car every four months or so. That would be pretty inconvenient, though. The autoworker might like a new car every four months, but how then would he buy groceries? How would he pay his electric bill? By sending a fender to the utility company?

Using money as a substitute for wealth allows the laborer to distribute his wealth in convenient amounts in order to acquire goods he needs and wants, like groceries and padded toilet seats.

How does non-productive labor get paid, though? They don't produce any goods, so they create no wealth to share. So why give them money? Well, the reason is that they provide services that a complex economy needs. Let's say the autoworker needs his house painted. He can't do it himself because he's making cars eight hours a day. So he hires a painter. In other words, the autoworker willingly gives some of his wealth away to the painter, because the service the painter provides is valuable.

Some other non-productive laborers like policemen, or members of the military, are paid by various levels of government. The government taxes other laborers to pay for these services. Professional athletes are also non-productive laborers. They produce no goods, and they don't have a service to offer. But other laborers are willing to pay them just to watch them play a game. So, while the creation of wealth is the basis of our economy, services are an important component as well, because they go beyond supplying our needs, and taking care of our wants. Services provide a way for us to have things done that we can't conveniently do for ourselves.

Division of Labor

In the largest sense, the division of labor is simply people doing all kinds of different jobs.

Once upon a time, almost everybody was a farmer. Since everybody had to farm all the time there was no entertainment industry. That made Saturday night TV very boring.

But slowly, people began to realize that if one group of people farmed, another group of people could build farm equipment, another group of people could process the farm products into food. That way, they would all have to work less individually, but they could produce more collectively. Because people produced more, they had more money. Because they worked less, they had more time for leisure. When society reached the point where it could enjoy some leisure time, and had become sufficiently rich, an entertainment industry arose.

Saturday night TV isn't much better, though.

One of the main benefits of division of labor is that it adds efficiency to the process of production. In *The Wealth of Nations*, Adam Smith provided the first example of how this efficiency is obtained by using the example of a pin-making factory. Pins are made up of two parts, the shaft, and the pinhead.

One way of making pins would be to have everyone assemble individual pins. Each person would have to make the pinhead, cut the wire to make the shaft, attach the pinhead, then sharpen the end of the shaft. This would work, but it is inefficient, because every person has to learn the entire pin-making process. Also, there is a lot of wasted activity, because each person has to switch to different tools to perform different parts of the process.

A more efficient way of making the pins would be to have one person make the pinheads, one person make the shafts, one person attach the pinheads, and another person to do the sharpening. By using the division of labor this way, each worker could specialize in one facet of production, and become more efficient. Much of the wasted activity that comes from having to constantly switch to different types of tools is eliminated. In effect, the division of labor allows an assembly line to be set up, with a continuous flow of pins moving through the process.

Imagine how difficult it would be to make a complicated piece of equipment, like an automobile, without the division of labor. If every car worker had to make one entire car at a time, it would take much longer to build each car. And imagine how long it would take to train each worker how to build a whole car! Every worker would have to know everything about how cars are built. With the division of labor, each worker only has to specialize in one thing. Training costs are lowered. More cars can be produced, because assembly line processes can be used.

Without the division of labor, producing almost anything would take far longer than it should.

PRICE [1]

Basic Functions

Let's go back and re-examine the three basic questions we asked when we defined what economics was:

1) What will we produce?
2) How will resources be used in that production?
3) Who will consume the goods we produce?

There are really only two ways that we can go about answering these three questions. We can create a market system, in which consumers and producers can determine these things among themselves, or we can create a command system, in which some group of policymakers address these questions.

In a market system, prices play the key role in determining how those questions are answered. Many people think of prices as a barrier to getting what they want. Other people assume that prices are a cost

---

1.   I am indebted to Thomas Sowell's *Basic Economics*, 2000, Basic Books, New York, for many of the examples used in this section, upon which I have expanded. His discussion of prices there is perhaps one of the best available for clarity and brevity.

imposed by producers in order to make a profit. In reality though, prices deliver information about the underlying realities of the market. They are not some arbitrary figure set by The System to rip us off, man. They are the primary way the market has of telling us the true state of supply and demand.

Let's take our bikini condo for an example again. There's only so much beach. Far more people want to live near the beach than there is beach in existence. So, when a lot of people start trying to buy beach-front bikini condos, the price will skyrocket. That price is telling us that there isn't enough beachfront property to go around.

This is a very important distinction. Many people see the price as the barrier to getting a beachfront condo. But the price *isn't* the barrier. The barrier is the physical lack of available land. All the price does is give us a signal that the amount of land is very limited.

The Federal Government may come up with a plan to provide beachfront condos for everyone. The Supreme Court may declare beachfront condos to be a basic right of all Americans. But there is still a limited amount of beach, and all the government action in the world won't change that physical limit.

Sometimes, of course, prices signal news that we like. Color TVs are cheaper than they were just a few years ago. Even prices for those new, high-definition plasma TVs are declining. As technology, management, or business practices improve, producers are able to increase the supply of goods. This causes prices to decline.

For example, I have more computing power in my Handheld PC than those string-tied, crew-cut nerds at Sperry-Univac could even dream about in 1955. And their computer was a 4-story laboratory that needed 30 tons of air conditioning to keep the building from melting from the heat of all the vacuum tubes. So, apart from having almost no computer power as we understand it today, a Univac was also pretty difficult to fit into a belt pouch.

My iPaq cost $400. Want to take a guess at how much the first Univac cost? Let me give you a clue: the *government* had to help pay for it.

Prices are also very efficient at conveying this information. Every time a new natural resource is found, or a radical new production method is devised, prices immediately begin to change to reflect the new reality. For example, what do you think would happen to the price of oil if the physics boys at Harvard announced they'd figured out how to produce cold fusion, or a cheap way of producing hydrogen?

As people began canceling long-term oil contracts in anticipation of new technologies, the price of oil would begin to decline. When GM started delivering the new Hydromatic Sedan to showrooms, owners of filling stations would begin leaving the business. Before you know it, the Saudis would be paying us to rid their country of that cursed petroleum.

Boy, what I wouldn't pay to see that.

Prices also guide producers as well as consumers. Sometimes, you'll hear someone arguing that a producer is "setting" prices for a product. It's just that greedy capitalist mentality, man, sucking the life out of The People.

But, how likely is this? I mean, I see businesses shut down all the time. Are you saying that all a business has to do is raise prices to a profitable level, and watch as the money comes rolling in to their Scrooge McDuck money vaults?

I don't think so.

The whole trouble with arguing that producers can "set" prices is that, in a market economy, all transactions are voluntary. If you don't like the price one producer sets on a product, you can buy from a competitor, or you can find a substitute. In the real world of competition and free choice, the ability of producers to set prices is almost nonexistent.

You may have noticed that sometimes a product—maybe even a product you like—suddenly disappears from the market. Well, just because you liked it, doesn't mean anyone else did.

I know. I had a Pontiac Aztek.

In a case like this, a manufacturer doesn't have much of a choice. If they want to have any hope of recovering some of their production costs, they have to reduce prices in the hope that consumers will buy their hideous trinkets at a discount. Yes, they will lose some money, but they don't really have much of a choice. Their only alternative is to lose everything by not selling the items at all.

The free market is not just a profit system, but rather a profit and *loss* system. Losses signal producers to lower prices, or face the possibility of going out of business.

To producers, prices signal the underlying reality about how consumers feel about their products.

Another feature of the price system is that it forces producers to put resources to their most valued uses. This is important because, quite often, consumers demand different goods that use many of the same components.

Let's take petroleum, for example. People don't just need gasoline; they need plastics to make computer keyboards and ugly furniture for college students. Businesses need chemicals for industrial production and dyes. Textile companies need artificial fabrics that don't fade or discolor. Perverts need Vaseline.

So, in bidding for each of those items, their producers are also bidding for the petroleum required to make them. When more people buy Vaseline, Johnson & Johnson has to bid away some of that petroleum from refineries or textile mills. In turn, this increased demand in petroleum causes the price of oil to rise for everyone who uses it.

In order to keep buying oil, everyone now has to pay the price that Johnson & Johnson is willing to pay. As this raises consumer prices for these items, consumers are likely to buy less of them. For example, a consumer, noticing the increase in the cost of Vaseline, decides to spend Saturday night alone.

So, the price that Johnson & Johnson is willing to pay for oil becomes an added cost for all of the other businesses that use oil. If they want to bid away some of that oil, they have to be willing to pay the higher price. But since higher prices tend to mean lower sales, other producers will only bid away as much oil as they think they can use, now that sales are dropping.

The end result is that Johnson & Johnson ends up with a relatively larger portion of oil. In other words, the resource of oil has flowed to the highest valued product, an important…uh…*medical* lubricant.

Eventually, because there is an increasing supply of Vaseline, demand is affected. At some point, consumers are unwilling to buy it, because there's enough of it on the shelves. And, of course, with all this petroleum bidding going on, the price has been increasing. So, some consumers may notice that the price of Vaseline has now increased relative to, say KY Jelly, and they may decide to purchase it instead.

Of course, either way, Johnson & Johnson wins.

But, this change in demand forces the company to produce less Vaseline, which means ordering less oil. Naturally, that frees up more oil for plastics manufacturers and chemical companies at a lower price.

In forcing resources to their most valued uses, prices provide an automatically self-correcting mechanism that adjusts the use of resources at all times.

Now, these adjustments in production are all incremental. It's not an all or nothing choice between Vaseline and gasoline. Each product has its own level of demand, and only the amount of oil necessary to make each product will be used. That prevents us from being unable to find a plastic travel cup for our coffee, but being flooded with enough Vaseline to film *Debbie Does Dallas* with the entire population of Dallas.

Since prices tend to push resources into their most valued uses, this means that the real price of any good is not a specific value. The price changes to match the conditions of supply and demand, and it always equals the value the item has when used in its most valuable, alternate use.

For example, let's look at the price of a college education in terms of this definition.

There is a price to going to college, and it's a lot greater than the 40,000 bucks or so it costs in tuition, fees and books. While you are going to school, you are probably not working in a full-time job. So, if you are working only 20 hours a week at a $6.25 an hour job instead of forty hours, you will also forego an extra $26,000 in income during those four years. This is also known as "opportunity cost". So the true price of a college education is $66,000 instead of $40,000, when you add in the opportunity cost.

Your time has alternate uses, even though you choose to use that time for study. By choosing study as the most valuable alternate use of your time instead of work, you forego thousands of dollars in income.

Next, prices serve as incentives for producers. If the price of oil increases, it serves as an incentive for oil producers to produce more, since it signals that more oil can be profitably bought to market. Low prices, of course, serve as a disincentive to produce, because they signal the underlying reality that oil is not as highly valued, and that consumers want less of it.

Indeed, those college grades you were working for a few minutes ago can also be thought of as prices, in that they provide incentives to behave in a certain way. For example, if you know that a good score on your final exam in Chemistry will guarantee you an A, then you might forego the *Unbearable Lightness of Being* film revival at the campus cinema, in order to study for a couple of hours.

Actually, you may want to forego that, any way.

Conversely, you might know that if you don't get a good score on the final you are guaranteed an F, so, again, you end up studying for those two hours. Either way, the price of your desired grade is two hours of study.

In the aftermath of Hurricane Hugo, construction workers from across the United States poured into Florida. They knew that there was going to be a huge demand for construction workers, and that they would make relatively higher wages working in the rebuilding effort, and that jobs would be freely available. They started showing up long before the state of Florida, or the FEMA boys from Washington, even had a chance to get organized.

The incentive of steady work and good pay due to the increased demand for construction poured those human resources into Florida in droves.

Value

When we say that prices reflect an underlying reality, we can think of it in the following way: Prices are a reflection of the value we place on a good or service. Value is determined by supply and demand, or, more simply, by how much a prospective buyer is willing to pay for it.

Let's say you own a 1985 Yugo that you want to sell. You decide you want to sell it for $40,000 and not a penny less. When prospective buyers start coming around, none of them are going to meet your price because your price is not a true reflection of the car's value. Not even if you've maintained it really well.

The only way anyone is going to pay you forty grand for fifteen-year-old Yugo is if they are incredibly stupid or certifiably insane. The value of the Yugo is probably a lot closer to $200, and sooner or later you'll have to lower the price to that level, or decide to let it just rust away in your driveway.

Either way, you're not getting the 40 grand.

The difficulty of being the seller or producer of any good is that you have to try and correlate its price with its value. Some people may be willing to pay $500 for the Yugo. Some will only pay $100. The value of the car is kind of vague. On the other hand, the price you put down as the seller has to be specific. You have to decide on a price that most potential customers will be willing to pay.

It's the same for the producer of any good. First you have to add up what it costs to make the goods you produce. Then you have to try to determine the value that customers will set on your goods—in other words, how much they're willing to pay. The goal is to set a price that is greater than the cost of making the goods, and is consistent with the value customers will put on them.

Let's take a look at new cars and see how pricing and value interrelate. Let's say General Motors makes the Chevrolet Caprice and the Pontiac Bonneville SSEi. The Caprice costs about $18,000. The Bonneville costs about $36,000. For all practical intents and purposes, they are the same car from GM's viewpoint. They use the same frame and body. They use many of the same parts. The workers who make them and the plants in which they are made cost about the same to run. The Bonneville is slightly more expensive for GM to make because it comes with more expensive interior appointments and a racier engine. Other than that, the difference between the two cars is mainly cosmetic. They are the same car. But the price of the Bonneville is more than double that of the Caprice. Why?

Customers value the two cars entirely differently. Customers see the Caprice as the car their grandfather drives. It's sedate. It's boring. It's respectable. It's middle class. It comes in tan, gray, white or black. It is utterly unexciting.

Aaah, but the Bonneville! A 225-horsepower engine! Excitingly chunky leather seats! A heads-up display that projects driving information right into your field of vision! A dashboard covered with knobs and dials and pretty lights! Flashy colors like British Racing Green! This isn't your grandfather's car!

So, a customer who would pay $16,000 dollars for the Caprice might do it as if he was doling out vials of his own blood. But that same customer would take one look at the Bonneville and toss out $36,000 in rolls of C-notes like a drunken sailor on Singapore shore leave just to drive that baby home.

The image the Bonneville provides adds a value that translates to an extra couple of thousand dollars of profit for GM. They can jack up the price of the Bonneville simply because people are willing to pay more for it. Between the Bonneville and the Caprice, the Bonneville has greater value.

Price Fallacies

Now, we often hear one of two fallacies about prices.

1) High prices are caused by greed

2) Something costs more than it is "really" worth.

For the first fallacy, we must understand that, as long as the market is free, and transactions are voluntary, the price is merely the vehicle for conveying information about the supply and demand for that product.

Sure, if I am selling widgets, I'm going to try to get as much for each widget as I can. Consumers, on the other hand, only want to pay as little as they can. In a free market, transactions are voluntary, so to sell any of my widgets, I must choose a price that buyers will voluntarily agree to pay, just as I did with my '85 Yugo, instead of asking for $40,000.

No matter how greedy I am for my 40 thou, the free market will not allow me to assuage my greed any more than consumers wish.

The second fallacy is that prices somehow don't reflect the "real" price for my goods. But, there is no "real" or "normal" value for any good. Prices reflect the relationship of supply and demand for goods at a particular point in time. Those goods may have been less valuable in the past. They may be more valuable in the future.

Over the past 100 years, farming has become vastly more productive. Hugely increased amounts of farm produce are available now. In fact, the supply of produce is so great, we are a net exporter of farm produce, which means we produce more farm products than we can actually use. At the same time, many people decry the "collapse" of farm prices, and demand that something be done to save the family farm, and return farm prices to their real level. But, since farm prices have been declining steadily for the past century, what is the "real" value of agricultural products?

As I was looking for houses last year, I noticed that house prices in Temecula, California were substantially lower than in the beachfront community of Oceanside. In Temecula, I could get a 3,000 square foot house for $220,000. But in Oceanside, that same price would hardly get me a house half that size. Which of those prices was the "real" price?

Well, both of them were. Temecula is inconveniently located out in the desert of southern Riverside County. Living there adds an extra half-hour of travel to work. And don't even talk about the traffic.

On the other hand, the climate is wonderful, if by "wonderful" you mean "like being spitted on an open fire".

Living in Temecula was cheaper because it's a less valuable place to live. The prices in both cities reflected the relative value of living there.

Rationing Function of Prices

Because all resources are scarce, they must be rationed. Prices change in response to supply and demand. By doing so, they direct resources to where they are most in demand, and direct people to where their desires can be most satisfied by the existing supply.

Oceanside, being a beachfront community, with pleasant weather, an ocean view, and easy access to highways and public transportation, is a more desirable place to live. A lot of people want to live there, but there simply isn't enough room to accommodate everyone. So the higher price of a home in Oceanside is the way that homes in that desirable area are rationed. The people in Oceanside aren't noticeably greedier than people elsewhere. They just live in an area where the demand for housing is high. The price just informs us of that underlying reality.

Prices can also move very quickly to reflect changes in that reality that affect the levels of supply and demand. Take a look at what happens when a natural disaster strikes. Homes are destroyed, and thousands of people have no place to live. When this happens, hotel prices suddenly shoot through the roof. Is this just naked, hideous greed? Well, perhaps, but what has really happened is that the supply/demand equation for living space has suddenly changed.

The suddenly higher price for hotel rooms is merely an example of prices performing the vitally important function of rationing. These resources are now far scarcer than the demand for them. Rationing is critically important in order to reduce the demand that each individual makes on these suddenly scarcer resources.

If those hotel prices stay the same, a family might be tempted to get two rooms, one for the parents, and one for the children. This deprives another family of that scarce resource. But if the prices shoot up drastically, then the same family is liable to share a single room, which means that another empty room is available for someone else's family.

Similarly, if the power goes out, people will need more flashlights. If the price of flashlights doesn't increase, families may begin hoarding flashlights and batteries so that every member of the family has their own. Higher prices for flashlights and batteries ration these purchases, so that fewer families are left without any flashlights at all.

Higher prices—rationing—forces people to share, even if they don't know that they are sharing.

There are, of course, other methods of rationing besides prices. One can ration on a "first come, first served" basis without changing any prices at all. The result of this rationing, however, is that larger numbers of people are left without any hotel rooms or flashlights. Alternatively, one can ration by fiat, that is, by ordering people not to hoard valuable items. Unfortunately, this type of rationing tends to be difficult to enforce, especially in emergency situations, making it relatively easy to evade.

No method of rationing is inherently more "fair" or "compassionate" than any other form of rationing. Rationing by price, however, is extremely efficient and hard to evade.

So, prices perform extremely important functions for the market economy:

1) They deliver information about the underlying realities of the current state of supply and demand.

2) They direct scarce resources into their most valued uses.

3) They provide incentives for producers.

4) They ration scarce resources.

SUPPLY AND DEMAND

The relationship between supply and demand is very simple. If people really want something you're selling, you can charge them through the nose. If they don't want it, you can't give it way at high noon in the town square.

Sometimes, just having a supply of something creates a demand where none had existed before. In economics, this is known as Say's Law, after the French economist Jean-Baptiste Say. Say's Law states: supply creates its own demand. This is a gross simplification of Say's Law, which we will discuss in slightly more detail later, but it sometimes provides an interesting insight into the way the market works.

A perfect example of Say's Law occurred back in the 1970's. It started when someone came up with a stupid idea. They took a rock, put it in a little cardboard carton, and stamped "Pet Rock" on the carton. It was amazing. Otherwise normal adults bought pet rocks, took them home, and proudly displayed them. An entire industry grew up around those things. There were pet rock care manuals. Books on teaching pet rocks to do tricks. Millions of these little suckers were sold! No one cared about pet rocks until there was a supply of them, and then everybody had to have them. The person who came up with this stupid idea became fabulously wealthy.

OK, maybe it wasn't such a stupid idea after all.

It all seems rather silly now, of course. Why did people want pet rocks? I don't really know, but people did take a lot of drugs in the '70s, so maybe that explains it.

The point is that the market forces of supply and demand are extremely powerful. In the case of the pet rocks, that power made the inventor of the pet rock very wealthy. But the effect can run the other way if you make a miscalculation. Sometimes, even the best run companies miscalculate the effects of those market forces.

In 1985, the Coca-Cola Company was in the middle of stiff competition for market share with PepsiCo. So the boys and girls at Coke decided they would change the formula for making their banner soft drink. They did long market studies and intensive taste tests in selected markets. They crafted a new Coca-Cola that beat their 100-year-old formula in taste tests. They prepared a sure-fire advertising campaign. And then, with as much fanfare as possible, they announced they were discontinuing old Coke and replacing it with a new, tastier beverage!

Bad move.

People hated it. They wanted old Coke. Stores had their entire supply of the original Coke bought within hours. A friend of mine bought 50 cases of old Coke, so he'd have some left when they stopped selling it. There were public demonstrations against the Coca-Cola Company. People bought new Coke just to pour it into the streets in protest. Pepsi sales soared.

Coca-Cola announced that they'd bring back the old formula under the name Coke Classic. Sales of Coke Classic skyrocketed. Distributors all over the country stopped stocking the new Coke. New Coke died a slow, quiet, lingering death. In 1995, the company announced it was discontinuing the new drink. Sometimes supply and demand can be vicious, but that makes the market very efficient.

In the two examples above, we see supply and demand in action. In one case, an essentially worthless product became a profitable money-maker—at least for a brief time—because people demanded huge numbers of it. In the other case, a popular product saw its demand collapse almost overnight, which was a complete debacle for one of the largest and most profitable companies in the world.

Naturally, it's pretty easy to see from these examples that supply and demand have a direct impact on prices. But the relationship can be complicated, because supply and demand are two independent things.

If the demand for a product increases, but the available supply remains the same, then prices will rise to reflect the increasing scarcity of that product. If demand remains the same, but additional supplies of a product are made available, prices will fall to reflect the decreasing scarcity of the product.

That's pretty straightforward, but what happens if both demand and supply increases? Or if both decline? The price will then fluctuate based on the relative scarcity of the product. If the demand for widgets increases 100%, and the supply increases by 50%, the product is still becoming scarcer. Hence the price will rise by the amount necessary to reflect the new relationship between supply and demand.

Remember, prices are not some arbitrary cost. They reflect the underlying reality about the state of supply and demand.

MONEY

So, now that we know about value and prices, it's time to look at the unit in which those two concepts are expressed. In the modern world, we express those concepts with money.

When an economic system is first getting started, people can trade goods that they make for other things they want. A farmer can give a butcher a certain amount of corn in return for a good porterhouse steak. A blacksmith can shoe the farmer's horses in return for some wheat. This is called the barter system, and it's still in effect in many poor parts of the world. But it only works up to a certain point. Eventually, the economy gets to be so complex that the barter system can't cope.

Barter is pretty inconvenient when you think about it. Let's say a farmer in a barter economy needed a new pair of shoes. The cobbler might not have wanted to accept a couple of bushels of wheat in return for a pair of shoes. After all, what was he going to do with it? He didn't have time to separate the wheat from the chaff, grind the wheat into flour, then bake the bread.

The only person who might have wanted the wheat is the local baker. But how was he going to pay the farmer? Let's say the farmer sold the baker enough wheat to make five hundred loaves of bread. Now, the farmer not only has enough bread to eat, he could use the bread to trade for a new pair of shoes.

Getting that new pair of shoes was still pretty inconvenient, though. What the cobbler really needed is a supply of small nails from the blacksmith. But the blacksmith didn't need a new pair of shoes every week. What the blacksmith needed was a steady supply of coal. The coal miner, however, could only use so many metal tools from the blacksmith. The coal miner needed torches to light the mine. The torch maker didn't really need coal, though. He needed bread. Unfortunately, the baker didn't really need too many torches.

All of these people needed something from each other, but they couldn't trade directly.

So the farmer had to get the baker to buy the wheat, and bake bread for the torch maker. The farmer could then buy torches with the bread. He could then trade the torches to the coal miner in return for coal. The coal went to the blacksmith in return for the little nails. Finally, he could trade the nails to the cobbler for new shoes. All the other members of this little barter economy shared the same problem the farmer had in buying his shoes.

Not only did this take up way too much time, everybody began to need several inconveniently large wagons to cart all this stuff around in when they went to 7-11 to buy a coke.

What everyone needed was a simple medium of exchange—something everyone wanted, with a generally agreed-upon value, which everyone accepted as payment.

That's where money comes in. Money becomes a substitute for all of these goods and services that the barter system just can't handle anymore. All you have to do is find a material that everybody will accept as valuable, and then you can trade your goods or services for that material. You can then trade it for anything you want. About 4,000 years ago, our ancestors realized that, and created money.

A couple of elements are required to create money.

The first requirement is deciding what material you're going to use as money. This is the actual medium of exchange.

The most common material used as money has been a precious metal, usually gold, silver, or copper. Even today, people buy and sell these metals because they are universally accepted as valuable.

Gold has generally been the precious metal that was widely used as money. Because gold is a very rare metal, the supply of gold has always been low. But since everybody has considered it valuable, the demand has been high. This interaction of supply and demand has generally made gold the most expensive of the "money metals".

Gold (or any precious metal for that matter) is actually a pretty neat form of money. It's durable enough to last for thousands of years. It can be cast into any weight or shape, so it can be made into ingots or coins of varying value. Even a small bit of it is worth a good bit of money (At the time of this writing, an ounce of gold costs about $400.00), so it can be conveniently carried around. Best of all, gold rarely loses its value. And even though almost every country now uses paper money instead of gold, you can still walk into almost any bank in the world, drop a bar of gold in front of the teller, and have it accepted as money.

It's really very neat stuff, and I wish I had a lot of it. Which reminds me, *don't* loan this book to your friends. Make them buy their own copy!

The next thing that has to be decided is the price of all the goods and services that the money will be used for. Under the barter system, a farmer might trade ten bushels of wheat for one windowpane. The price of a windowpane is then ten bushels of wheat per pane.

That doesn't change when money is used. A bushel of wheat is priced at ten cents and windowpanes are priced at one dollar apiece. So the price of one windowpane is still the same as ten bushels of wheat. All money does is express the price of goods differently; it doesn't change what they are actually worth. But it simplifies everything because you don't have to try and figure out the exchange ratio of every single good and service in the economy with every other good and service. All you have to do is decide how much money each good and service is worth.

Once you have money, the exchange of goods and services can become vastly more efficient. It makes the creation of new goods and services easier to integrate into the economy, as well, because you no longer have to figure out where a new product fits into some massively complicated barter scheme.

Money allows the creation of large, complex economies.

2

ECONOMIC PRACTICES

CAPITALISM

The US economic system is called capitalism. It's also called the free market or the free enterprise system. It's pretty simple. You can produce any good or service you want. If people like it, they'll pay you for it. If they don't like it, you declare Chapter 11 bankruptcy.

Capitalism organizes the whole society into a market. Everyone in the society is buying and selling to everyone else. You sell your labor to your boss. He buys it by giving you a paycheck. You buy your groceries with that paycheck. Everyone in the country is part of the market.

Why is our economic system called capitalism? Because the things needed to produce wealth are called capital. If you own a farm, your land is capital. If you manufacture goods, your factory is capital. If you build houses, your tools and machinery are capital. So, if you own a business that produces goods, you are a capitalist.

Capitalism has certain characteristics that make it a very effective economic system.

First of all, it encourages people to be innovative, and create new goods and services. If people want a certain good, they'll buy it. If you can make the type of good people want, they'll buy it from you, and you'll make money. Sometimes you'll make a lot of money. The possibility of making a lot of money encourages innovation. Capitalism rewards success. It appeals to greed. And that's a pretty darn powerful incentive.

Capitalism is, in many ways, self-regulating. If you make a product and the quality is poor, people won't buy it, and you'll go out of business. In a capitalist society, there is competition for almost every good. If you make a shoddy product, then General Electric will come along and make it better. And while GE is making millions of dollars by selling that product, you're talking to bankruptcy attorneys. That competition makes the market efficient, rewards the maker of good products, and punishes the maker of bad products.

One of the key features of capitalism is that it operates through a free market in which everyone in the economy buys and sells the things they want. It is a voluntary system. Hulking thugs from Ford Motors don't drop by the house and suggest to you that you old car's getting dirty, so maybe you should think about buying a new one. You buy a car when you want or need to, and you buy the model of car that best suits your needs.

This is a very important thing to remember, especially when you hear arguments about how income or wealth is "distributed" in society. The term "distributed" is a very tricky one. It implies that there's some sort of central authority, deciding who gets paid $10 an hour and who doesn't, or who gets to buy a car, and who gets a new boat.

In a free market, though, there is no central authority. The distribution of goods or wealth is the result of millions of people making private decisions every day about what to sell. The distribution of economic benefits in a free market is the result of an impartial and impersonal process, not the result of some leader or small cabal deciding who gets what.

Because the free market is not centrally controlled, economic inequities result. Not everybody gets the same rewards.

This upsets some people. One of the biggest political debates of the last two decades has been about how to equalize the differences between the rich and the poor. The problem, of course, is how to do this in a free society.

Economist Thomas Sowell has proposed the following thought experiment. Let's say we create a small society of 1,000 people, and give each person $100. Everyone in our society is completely equal in terms of wealth, and can spend their money on anything they'd like.

Now, let's say that one of the citizens of our new society is a gifted musician. He decides to hold a concert, and he will charge $10 for each ticket to hear it. If everyone comes to the concert, then at the end of the night, our musician will have $10,090, while everyone else in our society will only have $90.

Why, that means that the top 0.1% of our society controls more than 10% of all our society's wealth! It's unfair!

But is it, really?

Everyone voluntarily gave the musician $10. If they'd wanted to, they could have purchased other goods or services. Instead, they freely gave their money to the musician. By doing so, they have caused the distribution of wealth in our little society to become incredibly unequal. But, that inequality resulted from each person making a voluntary decision.

To understand this is not to argue that the inequality is either good or bad. But it's important to recognize that a free market system lacks any central control, which means that it cannot guarantee equal results. A person who provides goods and services the public values will receive more economic rewards than a person who doesn't.

As a result, the only way to reduce inequality in a free market is to limit the choices available to the market, or to confiscate some portion of the wealth of those who receive the most rewards. In other words, to limit the inequality that results from a free market, you must limit the freedom of those who participate in the market.

The discussion about whether or not you should limit freedom in order to reduce economic inequality is a political discussion, not an economic one. But make no mistake; it *is* a discussion about limiting the freedom of the market.

As a compassionate society, however, we may decide that taking care of the least fortunate members of society provides a social good that far outweighs the economic harm of minor interference in the market. Economics can't tell us whether or not we *should* make this decision, but it can tell us what the decision is likely to cost.

SOCIALISM

Socialism is the economic system that replaces the free market with a system designed to eliminate inequality.

At its most extreme, socialism prohibits the ownership of private property, centrally plans the production of all goods and services, and strictly controls the income of each member of society. In the old USSR, a state agency called GOSPLAN actually planned the output of every good and service in the country, mandated salaries for the workers, and set the prices of goods and services to the consumer.

A more liberal version of socialism, welfare-state socialism, allows the ownership of private property, has unplanned private enterprise, and no control of incomes. In these states, the economy is socialized through high and steeply graduated income taxes to ensure that income disparities are eliminated. The state's role is to collect income taxes, and redistribute that income through benefit payments or other programs like universal medical care.

In both cases, however, socialism requires the intervention of a central authority to at least ensure equitable distribution of all goods and services.

Drawbacks to Socialism

Socialism sounds like a good idea. Its stated purpose is to create a fair society where no one is extremely rich or extremely poor when compared to the rest of society. In actual practice, however, socialism accomplishes this by making society in general poorer than it would be under a free market.

Sweden is commonly touted as a successful socialist country. While Sweden does have a private market and private ownership of property, there are no great differences in wealth or income distribution, because Sweden redistributes wealth mainly through high levels of income taxation.

According to the Swedish Research Institute of Trade (HUI), the median household income for Sweden in 2001 was $26,800[1]. In the US, the figure was $39,400. In fact, Swedes had lower per capita income than even African-Americans, the poorest economic group in the US.

According to the Reuters news story about this finding:

> "Weak growth means that Sweden has lost greatly in prosperity compared with the United States," HUI's president, Fredrik Bergstrom, and chief economist, Robert Gidehag, said.
>
> International Monetary Fund data from 2001 show that U.S. GDP per capita in dollar terms was 56 percent higher than in Sweden, while in 1980, Swedish GDP per capita was 20 percent higher.
>
> "Black people, who have the lowest income in the United States, now have a higher standard of living than an ordinary Swedish household," the HUI economists said.
>
> If Sweden were a U.S. state, it would be the poorest, measured by household gross income before taxes, Bergstrom and Gidehag said.

And Sweden is considered a *successful* socialist country. It has a vibrant private sector, as well as a fair amount of economic freedom.

When the USSR and its eastern satellite states collapsed and abandoned communism, it quickly became clear that several decades of communist economics had been a financial, economic, and human

---

1.   This figure accounts for purchasing power parity, not just raw income.

tragedy for those countries. Their people were significantly poorer, and their environments had been disastrously degraded.

While there isn't enough space to delve into a complete critique of socialism, a brief survey of its drawbacks will help explain why socialist countries are markedly poorer that capitalist ones.

One of the key tenets of economics is that people respond to incentives. People tend to do things that reward them and tend not to do things for which they are penalized.

For example, if you were a college student, and I told you I would give you $1,000 if you made at least a "B" on all your final exams, would you study harder? Probably. That $1,000 might be worth an extra ten or twenty hours of study, to ensure you did well on your finals. But, what if I offered you $1 for getting the same grade? Would you study as hard? Probably not.

You respond to the incentive of $1,000 because it represents enough money to make an extra effort worthwhile.

Socialism's biggest drawback is that it eliminates incentives to be successful. No matter how popular or useful a new product is, the owner is prevented from enjoying extra income by having it confiscated by the state. What is the incentive to become a brain surgeon as opposed to a file clerk if the income you make will be roughly the same?

Becoming a brain surgeon requires quite an investment. You must spend 4 years in college. Then an additional 4 years of medical school is required. After that, there are another couple of years of internship and residency.

To become a file clerk, you must be literate.

So, what is the incentive to make the huge investment needed to become a brain surgeon?

In effect, socialism, by hiding the scarcity of resources, inhibits the proper action of the price mechanism. The services of a brain surgeon cost pretty much the same as a file clerk. But brain surgeons are far scarcer than file clerks.

This kind of price distortion has a significant effect on the ability of the economy to perform properly. Remember the four functions that prices serve:

1) Prices deliver information about the current state of supply and demand.

2) Prices direct scarce resources into their most valued uses.

3) Prices provide incentives for producers.

4) Prices ration scarce resources.

When prices are set artificially, they cannot perform these functions. Rational calculations about the true costs of goods and services remain hidden.

For example, socialized medicine hides the cost of health care from the patient. The patient pays his health tax, and then pops round to the doctor's office any time he has a sniffle. The demand for health care increases, because when everyone does this, it reduces the time doctors have for patients with more serious problems.

In a free market, the price of health care would rise as a result of this increased demand. People might decide to go to the drug store and pick up some cold medication rather than spend the money on a trip to the doctor. Increased prices force the consumer to ration his own health care, and to go to the doctor only when it's necessary.

But, since prices can't rise in a socialized system, they can't perform their rationing function. Eventually the increases in demand will force the government to either pay more for health care than it raises from health taxes, or to save costs by rationing health care through eliminating benefits.

No matter how socialism tries, it cannot eliminate the underlying reality of scarcity. But by masking that reality, socialism inevitably builds up hidden costs and inefficiencies that reduce the wealth of the economy as a whole.

To date, no socialist economy has managed to create as much wealth for its citizens as a capitalist free market economy. And that is not an opinion, it is a historical fact.

Communism and Totalitarianism

There is another historical fact that has to be faced, which is that the most extreme form of socialism, communism, has invariably been tied to repressive methods of government.

Communist governments the world over have, without exception, been totalitarian states. The worldwide death toll of communist states in the 20th century is estimated to be close to 200 million people. In the USSR, 20 million people were intentionally starved in the 1920s and 1930's as the Soviet government forcibly imposed the collectivization of agriculture on the populace. Mao's Great Leap Forward similarly caused the death of approximately 50 million people, and millions more were killed during the Cultural Revolution. Untold millions perished in the wastes of the Siberian *gulag*, or the "re-education" camps of Asia.

Why is it that Communism, with its calls for universal brotherhood and equality, has invariably ended up creating the most repressive, brutal regimes in modern history?

Some would answer that true Communism has never been implemented, and that the so-called "communist" states were perversions of the communist idea, not representative examples of it.

But if Communism is so prone to such abuse, that seems to indicate a fundamental weakness of communism as a scientific system, in that it contains too few safeguards for the rights of the people to prevent it from assuming a totalitarian character. Moreover, such an excuse fails to explain why, in direct contrast to communism, states with free-market economies have tended towards ever-greater political freedom and liberalization along with far higher standards of living for the populace as a whole.

It is, in fact, the very nature of the communist system itself that leads directly to totalitarianism, and the free-market system that leads to liberalization.

The system of free markets, or Capitalism, is based on the premise that mutually agreed upon transactions between a willing buyer and willing seller are the only reasonable basis for economic organization. It presupposes a rule of law that prohibits forced or involuntary transactions and that recognizes that the owner of a thing has the right to dispose of it without hindrance from others. Capitalism therefore operates under three premises:

1) Voluntary exchange of goods and services,
2) The right to property,
3) The rule of law.

Capitalism is not a managed system. It is, rather, a framework under which a self-governing system operates. There is no Central Committee of Capitalists that determines what goods should be produced, or who should receive X amount of income. Instead, the end result of the free market is determined by millions of people, each of whom makes voluntary exchanges of goods and services. The only way to profit in the free market is to provide a good or service others are willing to buy.

The key mechanism in the free market is the price mechanism. As we've seen, prices perform extremely important functions for the market economy. Because the price mechanism performs these functions, it is possible to make rational economic calculations. If we see that the public has a demand for some good or service that is not being fulfilled, we can go into business to provide it. We can calculate how many people we need to hire, how much office space would cost, and how many units we have to sell to make a profit.

Let's go back to our pet rock example. The creator had to figure out the costs of the rocks, the boxes and instruction books, the little fiber nest each rock would be placed in, and the labor to put it all in the box. By knowing his costs, he could then calculate the sales price for each pet rock. An effective price mechanism allowed him to make all of these calculations accurately.

Although, frankly, how any of this helped the pet rock guy figure out that there was a huge public demand for small stones in the first place is beyond me.

The price system only works, however, because of the ownership of private property. Every exchange of goods and services is an exchange of property. Because we use money as a proxy for property, we do not, say, have to pay a baker with a bushel of grain in order to obtain a loaf of bread. But the money is not a thing of value in and of itself. It is merely a medium of exchange that substitutes for bartering real property to obtain the things we need. If I own a quantity of land, and wish to sell it, it is not because I wish to obtain green bits of paper, but rather because I wish to obtain some other type of property, perhaps one of those cool Pontiac Azteks.

Under Communism, however, there is no private property. This has enormous political and economic consequences, which create a "feedback loop", with each reinforcing the other.

As a political matter, "the people" own all property in a communist society. Herein lies the first step towards totalitarianism. In anything other than the very smallest community, how can "the people" exercise the rights of ownership to anything?

One cannot, after all, hold a national referendum every time one wishes to find out whether a majority of the 280 million people in the country agree that 200 acres of land should be set aside to build the People's Red Banner Tractor Factory in Topeka, Kansas. As a practical matter, therefore, the ownership of all property is exercised by the State, rather than by "the people".

This provides the State with control over nearly every aspect of the citizen's life. The State can dispossess you from your home, since it is, after all, not your home to begin with, but merely the place the State allows you to live. The State can dismiss you from your job and, since the State must control all enterprises, can effectively prevent you from obtaining any employment at all. Indeed, if your job is no longer needed, the State can force you to do any job it requires, whether you wish to do it or not. The State can determine where—or if—you can go to school.

The central political problem in such a system then becomes how one restrains the State from usurping all of the people's political rights. Obviously, some democratic system must be used for selecting the government if one wishes to make the government responsive to the people and subject to civil audit.

But if there are no rights to private property, then there is a huge swathe of political ideas that automatically have to be removed from the judgment of the people. The people cannot be allowed to vote on whether they wish to have private property, for instance. Candidates that counsel a return to Capitalism cannot be allowed to run for office. In practice, this means that, at the very least, political freedom and democratic practice must be rigidly proscribed to a small range of acceptable political thought. At the very start, a freely democratic government is impossible in the communist State.

The only possible way that such a system can work is to ensure that elected officials are people of such outstanding moral capacity that they would never think of using the vast control wielded by the State for personal gain. Such politicians are not especially easy to find even in openly democratic societies where the government exercises far less control over property rights.

Moreover, it is not possible to elect the vast majority of people who work directly for the State. A system of bureaucracy is required to carry out the day-to-day operations of the government. Even in the US, bureaucrats are regularly decried as the perpetrators of all sorts of outrages. Remember the controversy over the high-handed actions of the IRS a few years ago? Are we to assume that the bureaucratic system in a State with such enormous power over everyday life, and where political dialogue is severely circumscribed, would be *less* oppressive?

Imagine a society where the State awards all jobs, and you are applying for a manager's position at the Glorious October Revolution Ball Bearing Factory #37. Your competition for the job is the wastrel son of a junior undersecretary at the Ministry for Ball Bearing Production. Will the factory manager choose you, the more qualified candidate, or will he choose the son of the person who determines whether or not he keeps his job as factory manager?

The key political weakness of Communism is that it devolves vast powers upon the State, then limits the democratic audit that the people can exercise, which leaves the people to depend upon the State to curb its own power.

The key economic weakness that follows from the abolition of private property is the lack of a realistic price system that can be relied upon to make rational economic calculation. If the ownership of private property is not allowed, then the range of voluntary economic transactions the citizen can make are severely circumscribed. One can purchase food, clothes, and other consumables, but no real property.

Prices in a Communist system cannot be set through the operation of supply and demand, because the State is the sole owner of all property, which leaves the State with a quandary about how to set prices. To understand the State's difficulty, let's say that you own three parcels of land. How do you sell parcel A to yourself? If you do manage to sell parcel A to yourself, what price do you charge for it in the absence of any real estate market? No matter what price you choose, it is an arbitrary price, as well as an artificial one.

The State's problem with this is multiplied manifold. Prices in a free market economy work two ways in delivering information to buyers and sellers. First, they aggregate information in the economy by reflecting the level of demand. Second, they funnel goods and services to their most highly valued uses. This is important because, quite often, consumers demand different goods that use many of the same components, and because prices reflect demand, producers can see at any given time what products the people most desire to buy, increasing production of that item, while reducing production for others.

Under the Communist system, however, prices are fixed by the State, rather than moving freely back and forth to reflect the changing nature of supply and demand. This means that the use of goods or services cannot flow to their highest-valued use, because the price system does not reflect reality. As a result, it is impossible to determine whether or not people need hammers or steel desks at any given time.

This means that rational economic calculation is impossible under communism. There is no way to determine at any particular point in time what goods should be produced, and where they should be delivered. The Soviet answer to this quandary was the "Five-Year plans" in which all economic production was centrally planned every five years. But such plans don't actually reflect current economic reality. At best, they approximate past conditions, since the planning for each Five Year Plan was based on the data gathered during the previous one.

As a result, products are delivered to the public with no real relationship to what the public wants or needs. Hence, the USSR's record of delivering things such as 5 reams of writing paper for every person per year, and 1 roll of toilet paper.

The second economic effect is the effect Communism has on labor. Ask yourself this question: Why do you work? In general, people work in order to acquire property. Most people, if given a choice, would prefer not to work, or at any rate to work far less, or in a much less structured environment. People work, in short, in order to consume.

It is not enough merely to have enough food on which to subsist, and enough shelter to escape intemperate weather. Humans have goals, a primary one of which is the acquisition of property. We enjoy having nice things. We save up money to buy houses, or boats, or cars. We work to provide things for ourselves and our families that we might not otherwise have. We work only because we derive benefits from doing so. Without those benefits, why would we work any more than was strictly necessary to eat and obtain shelter?

Under Communism, however, you are forbidden to own real property. You cannot start your own business. You cannot buy a house. You can't even redecorate your home, because it isn't yours. It belongs to "the people".

In addition, wages are controlled under Communism, since equality of condition is Communism's primary goal. How much work would you be interested in doing under such a system? Probably, the minimum necessary. And what kind of work would you do? If security guards and brain surgeons both get paid $500 a month, which job would you prefer? The one you can start now with no training, and no great responsibility, or the one that takes 8 years of college and an additional 4 years of on-the-job training?

Under communism, workers don't receive commensurate rewards for working longer, harder, or more productively. That has devastating effects on worker productivity. Since all wealth creation is based on productivity, that means society's ability to create wealth is hindered as well. That translates into lower living standards for the population as a whole.

As the old Soviet joke goes, "They pretend to pay us, and we pretend to work."

In the end, these economic problems feed back into the political system.

The results of an irrational system of production mean that at any given time, people suffer a shortage of a range of desired goods, and glut of undesired goods. Their work allows little room for self-improvement or advancement. In a democratic system, this naturally translates into a political demand for change.

In a Communist system, with necessarily narrow limits on acceptable political thought, and hence few institutional limits on government power, any political call for change is necessarily limited to "reform" of the communist system. But in a system where rational economic planning is impossible, so is reform. The only realistic reform is the abandonment, either partially or in substantial measure, of the communist system itself.

If the system cannot be reformed to any useful degree, and the abandonment of the communist ideal—and the concomitant loss of its authority—is unacceptable to the State, then as the demand for change on the part of the public increases, then the only response remaining to the State is the repression of dissent.

As a practical matter, therefore, the very nature of communism makes democratic governance impossible.

The Star Trek *Objection*

I've presented the section above several times, either in written form or in speeches. Invariably, whenever I do so, there is always at least one member of the audience who informs me that in the future, as portrayed by the television show, *Star Trek*, the economy is socialist. Indeed, there was recently a fairly widespread debate about this very objection on the Internet, among the community of web log writers known as the "blogosphere". I am often amazed that a simple TV show can rouse such passions about economics.

Before I begin to address that objection, though, I should tell you that I remember when the original Trek was on NBC. I remember playing with neighborhood friends at 4 years of age (1968), and deciding who was going to be Kirk, Spock, McCoy, and Scotty.

I also taught computer training regularly at Paramount Studios in Los Angeles while the *Star Trek* series *Deep Space 9* and *Voyager* were in production there, and I used to spend my lunches hanging around on the sets.

I think I have better than average Trek knowledge. You, on the other hand, may not be interested in this at all, so if you aren't a geek, you might just want to skip this bit and move directly to the next section.

In any event, as blogger Matt Yglesias[2] points out in advancing the "*Star Trek* is commie" argument"

> [I]t seems clear to me that Star Trek (at least in its The Next Generation form) advances a specifically Marxist view of politics. The idea is that, at some point in the future, technological progress driven by capitalist competition and innovation, will lead to the

---

2.   Quote taken from a daily web log entry.

invention of the replicator, thus bringing about Marx's "overabundance of goods" and leading to the collapse of market exchange as a viable means of social organization.

Well, as the Picard character once said on one of those *we're low on location budget so let's move over to the 20th century earth sets on the other side of the Paramount lot* episodes, "I'm afraid you would find the economics of the 23rd century rather difficult to understand." That's probably true about most people alive today.

All economics, even Marxism, is based in the concept of scarcity. Marx merely believed the value of a good or service consisted solely of the value of the labor required to transform raw goods into finished products. But the reason labor itself was valuable was because of scarcity. There is, after all, a finite number of laborers, meaning that the production of goods had to be allocated through the labor available to produce them.

What makes *Star Trek*'s economics fundamentally different, and, in many ways, fundamentally incomprehensible to us, is that scarcity is no longer a factor. In that universe, there is an invention called the "replicator" which can transform matter at the atomic level. Put in a rock, or, more likely, some cheap carbon slurry, and out pops bacon and eggs. Or a cup of Earl Gray, hot.

The invention of the replicator in the *Star Trek* universe means that essentially no good is scarce. Practically any physical good can be obtained at negligible cost, either through replicators, or through construction by artificially intelligent robots using replicator-produced prefabricated parts.

So imagine a universe in which your food, clothing, vehicle, home, and practically every other tangible good is essentially free, and in which energy can be obtained for free through your home's antimatter reactor.

Now, the reason we all have to drag ourselves out of bed Monday through Friday is to obtain the money we need to trade in exchange for goods and services. If we could have all those things for free would we actually work?

Probably not.

Still, we couldn't just sit on our bums all day without going stir crazy. Even constant sex with the "Claudia Schiffer" program in the rec room holodeck would get old after a while, as hard as that might be to believe. Human beings, in short, would still have needs.

But, as Abraham Maslow tells us, there is hierarchy of needs. Once we've taken care of physical needs, we still have social needs, and self-actualization needs. So, if you didn't have to work to survive, you would probably "work" at an avocation, doing things you love to do.

Would you even be paid for working? What would you buy with that payment, in whatever form it would take, that you don't already have for free?

I'd be perfectly happy to teach classes in computer science, economics, history and all sorts of other things that fascinate me. At other times, I would want to go to school, and learn about more things that fascinate me.

Frankly, I think the economics of such a society would be fairly hard to envision. For instance, how would the service economy work? If you were hit by an aircar, would you pay for a lawyer, or would there simply be people for whom litigation was a pleasure, and who would take your case for free, because they like litigating?

There would, of course, still be scarce things. Book collectors might still wish to obtain signed first editions of John Grisham novels. But that opens up a whole can of worms, too. How would they obtain them? There would have to be some medium of exchange, but what would it be? And, if you aren't particularly interested in formulaic legal novels written by long dead scribblers, what would you use that medium of exchange for, what with most other things being essentially free? If you own a first edition Grisham, what would I have to give you in order to obtain it for myself, if you already have everything else you want?

The replicator moves the debate well outside the capitalist-Marxist paradigm, into something largely unknown. I think a lot of trial and error would have to be done to come up with rational answers to these questions.

Star Trek also includes a voraciously capitalist alien race known as the Ferengi, who make an interesting case in this context. I mean, they're just completely amoral free-marketers. They have a whole society ruled by the *Sacred Rules of Acquisition*, their holiest text.

But, they have replicators as well, and as many Claudia Schiffer holo-wives as they could want. So why all the unregulated capitalism?

Well, in their case, it appears to be a cultural deal. They don't want all that "gold pressed latinum" to ease them in their old age. They already are fantastically rich simply because they have replicator technology.

But the number of latinum bars one has is a good way to keep score. The higher the number of gold-pressed latinum bars one has, the higher their social status. If they've managed to obtain the latinum by hoodwinking someone else for it, their status is increased even more.

"Wealth" in the Ferengi sense has negligible economic value, but immense social value. It serves a *cultural* purpose, even if it no longer marks extreme differences in economic status. Indeed, the ownership of "riches" has a significant place in how the Ferengi organize their political structure, since obtaining riches is taken by their culture to be a prime indication of good judgment and fitness to lead.

So, even the Ferengi are not quite what they appear on the surface.

And Star Trek's economics aren't as Marxist as many people seem to think, either. Without scarcity, there's no Marxism at all. Apart from anything else, there's no proletariat. So, while there may be objections to my argument that communism is inherently totalitarian, it can't be found in *Star Trek*.

Oh, yeah, and *Star Trek*'s not real.

THE COMPLEXITY OF THE MARKET

So far we've just looked at a few of the basic principles of economics. In real life, things are much more complex. These simple principles are playing out in the lives of all 280 million Americans every day. Anything that has 280 million moving parts is bound to be extraordinarily complex, and the US economy is no different.

First of all, there are very many different types of jobs to be done. There are literally thousands of different occupations that have to be done every day just to keep the economy moving along. Changes in just one of those different occupations may affect the economy of the entire nation as a whole.

Government also plays a roll. Government policies on spending, taxation, and regulation determine how much money is available in the economy to build things and hire workers. If the government changed the tax brackets tomorrow, and you were suddenly in the 60% tax bracket, how much money would you have left after taxes to buy things? If the government decided the minimum wage should be increased to $35 per hour, how many businesses would have to close because they couldn't afford to pay their workers?

Government is an enormous force in the economy, because it can change the very ground rules about how business is conducted.

International events also play a role.

In 1973, several Arab nations attacked Israel. The US supported Israel by airlifting in all sorts of military supplies. The Israelis won (again). The Arab countries didn't like losing, and they certainly didn't like our support of Israel, so they got back at us.

They decided not to send oil to the US. The price of oil shot up to outrageous levels as the supply could no longer meet the demand. Gas stations ran out of gas, and had to ration every shipment they got. Lines at stations that had gas stretched for miles.

With the price of gas so high, it became more expensive for utility companies to provide power, which meant rates went up. That meant that every product that required energy to produce became more expensive. Inflation shot up to double-digit numbers. The embargo itself was brief but the effects lasted for the second half of the decade. And things weren't helped by the fact that, when the Arab countries did decide to sell gas to us again, the price had more than tripled by the end of the 70s.

Weather can play a part in the economy, too. What if corn blight destroyed every ear of corn in Iowa? Corn would start getting pricey. The California floods of 1995 destroyed a large portion of the nation's lettuce, broccoli, and other agricultural goods. The price rose as a result.

The complexity of the economy is made even worse by the existence of the business cycle.

THE BUSINESS CYCLE

For some reason, economies seem to go through periods of growth and recession. No one can completely explain why it happens. Take the great depression that started after the Wall Street Crash of '29. No one has ever explained exactly why the economy went belly up, and that was 60 years ago.

Well, actually, a lot of them *have* explained it; the problem is that they all disagree with each other.

What we do know is that every period of expansion in the economy is followed by a period of recession. The recessions don't usually erase all the gains made during the expansion. It's kind of a case of two steps forward and one step back. Since the end of World War Two we've gone through the business cycle ten times.

The terms expansion and recession are related to the country's Gross Domestic Product, or GDP. The GDP is the measure of all the goods and services created by the economy. We measure whether the economy is in expansion or recession by looking at the growth rate of GDP. If the GDP is growing, we are in an expansion. If the GDP is shrinking, we are in a recession. In a mature economy like the US, the GDP will rise about 3% to 4% over the previous year during an expansion. During a recession, GDP will decline to a level that is about 1% to 2% lower than the previous year.

During an expansion, the economy grows, more businesses start or expand, and unemployment drops as more jobs become available. For a variety of reasons, prices tend to rise near the end of the expansion. During a recession, businesses close, unemployment rises, and prices tend to fall.

Economists are divided about why the business cycle exists. Actually, economists are divided about a lot of things, so the last sentence shouldn't really be a surprise. Some say that large economies are unstable, so they move in fits and starts. Others say that outside interference in the operation of the market is to blame.

Whatever the reason, economists and government policymakers have been trying to find a way to moderate or even eliminate the business cycle. So far they haven't been very successful. Since 1948 the score has been: Business Cycle 9, Economists 0.

In 1978, Congress passed the Humphrey-Hawkins bill. The bill included a five-year plan to eliminate budget deficits, eliminate inflation, bring the unemployment rate to as near zero as possible, and then keep it there for the foreseeable future. Of course, you remember how in 1983 the budget was finally balanced, everybody had a job, and prices for everything in the country stopped rising.

You don't remember that? Well, that's because the law didn't work. For some reason, the economy just seems to do what it darn well pleases.

Frankly, the economy is so complex, and so subject to non-economic forces, that no one really understands it totally. So, every time we try a nostrum like Humphrey-Hawkins, it fails. Trying to regulate the business cycle in an economy as complex as ours is very difficult, perhaps even impossible.

But it's always comforting to know that government officials have the guts to go on trying, even if they don't understand a darn thing about how to do it. That's the kind of can-do attitude that made this country great.

MONOPOLIES

From an economic point of view, a monopoly is said to exist when:

a) A single firm or a very few firms provide the all or a great majority of products or services available from an industry.

b) There is a high barrier that prevents other firms from entering the industry on a competitive basis.

There are essentially two types of monopoly:

a) A market monopoly exists when a company creates a monopoly in a free market.

b) A legal monopoly exists when a company is granted monopoly power by government regulation or law.

Monopoly, as a legal concept in antitrust law, begins to come into play mainly when there are allegations of:

1) The ability to set consumer prices at higher levels (e.g., through restricting output.)

2) The ability to eliminate competition (e.g., predatory pricing, restrictive contracts with retailers)

3) A reduction in the quality of goods.

There can be any number of perfectly benign reasons why a monopoly exists. For example, a product might have such a limited market that very few companies are able to service it (a natural monopoly). Or perhaps the natural barrier to entry in an industry is so high that few companies are willing to enter it. One company may simply be able to produce more efficiently than any potential competitors. So, in some cases (and certainly in the cases of a natural monopoly), a monopoly may simply be a fact that must be lived with, rather than a problem that has to be solved.

In fact, it may be that way in almost all cases of market monopolies. Let us look at the three dangers of monopoly that are addressed by antitrust law.

The ability to Set Prices

This assumes that producers actually have the power to set prices. It is by no means clear that this is true.

First, most market monopolies (i.e., those created by market competition, rather than by government intervention or regulation) became so by lowering the prices paid by consumers to levels which their competitors could not meet.

Standard Oil had absolute control over its oil from production, to refining, to retail sale. Its competitors did not. Standard Oil became a monopoly because it introduced an entirely new business model: the Integrated Oil Company. This new business model was far more productive, because it eliminated the artificial divisions between exploration, production, refining, and retail sales, and combined them into a single company. Other competitors who did not have this integrated structure were less productive, and could not compete.

So, Standard Oil's monopoly actually benefited consumers by lowering the price, increasing the availability, and increasing the quality of petroleum products.

Second, there is relationship of demand to price. Price and demand are inversely proportional. Any producer that raises prices must deal with the fact that higher prices reduce demand. Consumers may substitute other products, or they may do without. This is called the substitution effect.

For instance, in an industry like the airline industry, margins are already quite thin. Raising prices carries with it the danger that reduced demand will actually cause profits to fall as consumers switch from the major airlines to small, regional concerns, or to trains, or to driving, instead of flying. The higher the price, the greater this substitution effect becomes.

American Airlines does not hold a gun to your head and make you pay for a ticket. American Airlines merely offers a ticket for sale at a certain price. Let us assume that American and United even get together and "collude" to fix a price. This does not repeal the substitution effect. There are other ways to get to your destination. Moreover, if, in fact, the public does not seek alternative methods of transport, then we may assume that the higher price is acceptable to consumers, who are, after all, making free choices about their travel.

Now, a monopoly could raise prices, and at the same time, lower output to match the decreased demand at the higher price. The trouble with this scenario is that it assumes that the threat of competition is nonexistent. But, even with high barriers to entry, monopolies have never been able to maintain a competition-free environment for anything but a very short length of time.

Montgomery-Wards had to deal with new competition from Sears; A&P with Safeway; AT&T with WATS, MCI and Sprint. Once a monopoly raises prices and reduces output, the incentive for other companies to enter the monopoly market increases.

The Ability to Eliminate Competition

Unlike some characters—whose names often end in vowels—in popular movies and television programs, businesses do not eliminate competitors by dumping them in the East River. Businesses eliminate competition by offering products and services to consumers at a lower price. If the competing firms cannot do so, then they may be driven out of business. This is, of course, precisely what is supposed to happen. Uncompetitive firms must either become competitive, or go extinct.

The market is not a vast charity whose purpose is to force consumers to subsidize uncompetitive firms. To enforce this type of "competitiveness", consumers would be required by law to pay higher prices so that uncompetitive firms could be protected. So, we would be left with a situation in which consumers are forced to pay higher prices to prevent the creation of a monopoly that might charge higher prices.

Huh?

In the most famous modern example of this argument, the Microsoft antitrust case, the argument was made that Microsoft was engaging in tactics to eliminate competition by the contracts it signed with computer manufacturers. To get a license for the Windows operating system, manufacturers had to pay a license fee for every computer they sold, even if it did not have the Windows operating system installed. As a result, manufacturers did not produce computers using the OS/2, Geos, UNIX, Solaris, or other operating systems. IBM, Sun, and others used this as a basis for an antitrust complaint against Microsoft.

But, computer manufacturers were free to reject such a deal, and use an alternative operating system. They were similarly free to install competing operating systems and charge higher prices for those systems. But they did not do so, and it is important to look at why this might be true.

It wasn't because threatening, squinty-eyed, computer programmers from Microsoft came into the plant and speculated loudly about how bad it would be if a fire broke out. It was because the manufacturers realized that there was insufficient demand for any other operating system. The market demand, for better or for worse, was almost entirely a demand for Windows.

As such, forgoing such a contract, or trying to market systems with Sun Solaris installed, was not economically feasible. These contracts reflected market realities, and Microsoft's intent is irrelevant. Had a sufficient demand for, say, OS/2 existed, manufacturers would have told Microsoft to engage in airborne coitus with the moon, or alternatively, with themselves.

Indeed, IBM, a former monopolist itself, tried to push the OS/2 operating system in competition with Windows, when Microsoft decided to disband their partnership. So, how many people reading this are using OS/2 on their computer?

Uh-huh. That's what I thought.

In fact, I would argue that the computer operating system market is a natural monopoly, because of the efficiencies inherent in having a single standard operating system in use. Adhering to a single standard reduces costs for training, software development, maintenance, and a host of other factors. Microsoft employees might have the hearts of angels and still have a monopoly because of the objective requirements of the user community.

A Reduction in the Quality of Goods

Another often-heard argument against monopolies is that, once a monopoly has been established, its owners tend make cheaper, shoddier goods in order to increase the profits they extract from a captive market.

Aside from the fact that this argument also assumes that there is no substitution effect, it also conflicts with the actual history of monopolies in the United States. The way firms have historically become market monopolies in the US has been to provide better goods and services at a lower price. Standard Oil got its name because John D. Rockefeller decreed that all products bought from Standard Oil anywhere in the country would *be* standard. The quality would be reliably high, simply because Standard had produced it.

Monopolies that raise prices or reduce quality are all subject to the substitution effect. Moreover, these activities tend to bring new entrants into the market, even if the cost of entry is quite high. The high cost of aircraft, for example, did not prevent Southwest Airlines or AmericaWest from entering the airline business. Even high barriers to entry can be overcome.

In any event, market monopolies have *not* historically reduced quality.

So, then what the heck *have* they done?

For the most part, market monopolies appear to be transitory phenomena. Indeed, it is difficult to point out a historical example of one that lasted longer than a decade (In the case of legal monopolies, they have lasted for decades and, indeed, are still with us). Even the case against Standard Oil, which is the classic antitrust action, Standard Oil's control of the domestic petroleum industry had declined from 96% of the industry at its peak, to 85% of the industry at the time antitrust action was initiated by the US Government.

Monopolies that do persist tend to be legal monopolies created through government activity, such as regulated utilities, cab companies, etc. In those cases, the barrier to new entry is impermeable because the law sanctifies it. So, competition*is* reduced, productivity *does* decline, output*is* lowered and prices*are* raised. The behavior of legal monopolies displays all of the monopoly evils that we are taught to fear. Yet, oddly enough, there tends to be little political pressure for political leaders to abolish the laws and regulations that create such monopolies.

It is difficult, however, to find an example of a market monopoly implementing the evils described above. Indeed, it is nearly impossible to find an example of a market monopoly that even managed to survive for any appreciable length of time.

Once a monopoly is established, the incentive for new firms to enter the market appears to be historically irresistible. By doing so, these new firms attempt to undercut the monopoly in price and/or quality, in an attempt to fill the natural demand for the monopolized service or product.

For the most part, monopolies have historically been unable to resist these new entrants effectively. The monopoly firm tends to become less efficient over time, and less able to adapt to changing market conditions. A&P, for example, after two decades as the largest grocer in the US (reaching 54% of the market), was unable to respond to new competition from Safeway. I'm not even sure there are any A&P Grocery stores left. I haven't seen one since 1982.

As a result of all these items, the economic community is increasingly coming to the position that anti-trust law is probably far less necessary than previously believed.

3

THE 800-POUND GORILLA

THE GOVERNMENT: WHO ASKED THEM TO BUTT IN?

The government is the biggest single player in the economy. Through its control of taxation and spending (fiscal policy) or its control of the money supply and interest rates (monetary policy), when the government sneezes, everybody else gets a cold.

The government didn't really start intervening in the economy until this century. Economic meddling began about the turn of the century, as the government began to try to correct inequities that grew out of the unregulated capitalism of the Industrial Revolution.

When we began to make the change from a rural, farming society to an urban, manufacturing society, inequities began to spring up. One of the drawbacks of capitalism is that it doesn't offer much in the way of social policy. Some people get very rich and others get very poor. This was especially noticeable around the turn of the century when factory workers—many of whom were just children under ten years old—were forced to work 12 hours a day for six days a week. The wages were terrible. Whole families sometimes had to work, or they would starve.

Naturally, the people who owned the factories were quite well off. They were making products as cheaply as possible, and selling them for as much as they could get. The efficient rules of the marketplace were in full force.

But, slowly, the government began to look at conditions in the factories. The public became aware of how women and children were exploited, and they were disturbed. So, laws began to be passed to regulate the labor market. Child labor was especially regulated. The government had taken the first steps toward moderating the social consequences of unregulated capitalism.

It was the Great Depression of the 1930's that really got the government involved in the economy, however. The Great Depression remains the worst economic crisis the United States has yet had. There had been economic crises in the past, but in those earlier crises, most people lived on rural farms and were relatively self-sufficient. They affected the financial centers and the cities, but were only minor inconveniences for most Americans.

The Great Depression was different. For the first time, a huge proportion of Americans lived in cities. The number of farms was dwindling. America was in the middle of the greatest economic transition of her history, and the Depression hit right in the middle of it.

First came the stock market Crash of 1929. The value of companies on the New York Stock Exchange went right into the dirt. The economy started to come unhinged as businesses closed and people began to be forced out of work. To top it all off, farms in the southern part of the Midwest were hit by a horrible drought. In 1933, banks began to fail, prices collapsed, companies went out of business, and the unemployment rate hit 25%. It was if everything that could possibly go wrong, did. It was Murphy's Law in action.

Then came the presidential campaign of 1932. Up until then the Republicans had been running the government. That all changed. In 1933, Democrats came sweeping into power, led by Franklin Delano Roosevelt, the new president. His administration pushed through all sorts of economic programs, especially after the Great Depression hit in full force in 1933. He started the social security system, along with a variety of other programs to try to use the government's power and money to stimulate the economy.

Whether Roosevelt's programs actually worked or not, they began the political practice of using government power and money to influence the direction of the economy. Since then, the government has become an important part of the economy and whatever happens in Washington affects all Americans—usually in their pocketbooks.

FISCAL POLICY

Government does not create wealth. It can't, really, because the government produces nothing. Apart from anything else, that means it doesn't have anything to sell. So, the government has to get money from somewhere else.

In modern times, the government has decided to get that money from us in the form of income and other taxes. Every paycheck has a bit deducted from it. Every business has to send in money every three months in estimated taxes. Then, on every April 15th, the government settles up with everybody.

If they've taken more than we actually owed in taxes, they send it back to us. If we haven't paid enough, we have to send in the rest of what we owe. All of the money that the government takes in every year is called revenue. The government uses those revenues to pay its expenses.

And the government has a lot of expenses. In 2003, the government had more than $2 trillion dollars worth of expenses. A lot of that money goes towards boring stuff, like the salaries of government employees. Some of it goes to stuff the conservatives want, such as ensuring the Defense Department has the ability to kill lots of foreigners. Some of it goes to things the liberals like, such as welfare checks to unwed, unemployed, teenaged mothers who've dropped out of high school.

Everybody gets a little piece of the pie.

Taxation

But all that spending has to come from somewhere. So the government has to tax all of us to get that money. Even though the government produces nothing, it can pretty much take what it wants in the way of taxes. By taxing, the government can slow economic growth by taking money directly out of our paychecks. Or it can cut taxes, and give us all a little extra money to spend.

There are actually several different types of taxes. The income tax is a tax whose amount is based on your yearly income. A tariff is a tax that is paid on the price of a good that is imported to the US. An estate tax is the amount of money you must pay the government out of the inheritance your crazy aunt left you. A property tax is the amount you must pay the government because you own land or a home. A sales tax is a tax you pay whenever you buy a product.

Frankly, there are a lot of taxes.

The purposes of taxation can be many and varied.

First and foremost, taxes are used to keep the government running. Taxes pay the salaries of the bureaucrats who write federal regulations determining the proper size of pits in "Grade A" cherries. Taxes pay for the self-serving junk mail you get from your congressman. Taxes also pay for the people at the DMV to do whatever is they are supposed to be doing but aren't doing whenever you're there.

Taxes are also used as fiscal policy instruments, to slow down or speed up growth, or to encourage savings and investment in different areas of the economy. For example, the current tax code allows people to put $2,000 a year into individual retirement accounts, tax-free. That means your taxable income is lowered and you pay less in income taxes. It is an encouragement to save.

Taxes can also be used to redistribute wealth. If rich people pay high taxes, and the government gives money to poor people, they are, in effect, transferring wealth from the rich to the poor.

Finally, taxes can be used to engineer social policy. If the government wants to stop people from drinking and smoking, it can levy "sin taxes" on alcohol and cigarettes, by taxing booze at $20 a bottle and $3 for a pack of smokes. (Actually, in the real world, people start buying these things on the black market, but that's another story.)

The US government taxes incomes at an average rate of about 28%–36% depending on how much money you make. Corporate income taxes are 33%. But, the tax code contains a maze of exemptions and deductions that take a lifetime of work to understand fully. As a result, many people pay much less than the percentages shown above.

A general rule to remember is that if the government taxes more, the economy tends to slow down, because the government is taking money out of the economy. That means businesses have less money to spend on hiring new workers, or building new factories, and consumers have less money to spend on Pontiac Bonnevilles.

On the other hand, if the government taxes less, then workers have more money to spend and businesses have more money to build more factories and hire more people. The economy tends to expand if taxation drops.

This is where tax policy begins to get tricky. If the government needs more money, the logical answer is to raise taxes so that revenues will rise. But, when taxes are raised, the economy tends to slow down. Because of the slowdown in the economy, revenues tend to drop because less economic activity means less tax money actually gets paid.

An economist named Arthur Laffer provided the best illustration of this problem. Laffer, being a good economist, created a graph to show how changes in the tax rate affect government revenues. (Those economists just love their little graphs.)

This graph, which is called the Laffer Curve, displays the amount of revenue the government receives as tax rates change. If the government charges no tax at all, government revenues are $0. As the government raises taxes, revenues start to rise as well, until they reach the Equilibrium Point. The Equilibrium Point is the tax rate that produces the highest amount of revenues.

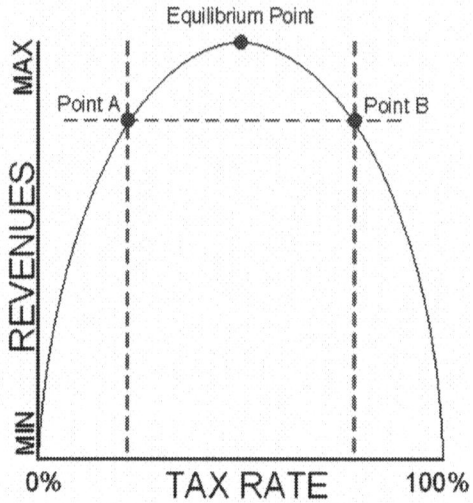

Figure 1: The Laffer Curve

After the equilibrium point is reached, revenues do not rise when tax rates rise. Instead, revenues begin to drop as tax rates rise, until, at the 100% tax rate, the government again makes no revenue whatsoever. With a tax rate of 100% there is no economic activity, because the government makes it pointless by taking away all of the profit.

The key feature to remember is that, except for the tax rate at the Equilibrium Point, there are two rates at which the government recovers the same revenue. Point A on the curve provides exactly the same revenue as point B, even though the two tax rates are quite different.

You may notice that the Laffer Curve doesn't actually pinpoint what the equilibrium point is. That's because the equilibrium point is constantly changing depending upon a wide variety of circumstances. For example, if everyone in the country was very poor, no one would be able to pay much in the way of taxes at all, because they wouldn't have enough money for food or shelter. In that case the equilibrium point might be quite low. On the other hand, if everyone were very rich, the equilibrium point might be much higher, because higher tax rates wouldn't have much effect on everyone's standard of living.

Even though it doesn't specifically identify where the equilibrium point is, the Laffer Curve does show that, after a certain point, raises in the tax rate are counterproductive, both in terms of the revenue gained by the government, and the slowing of general economic activity.

So, what is the equilibrium point in the US economy as far as tax rates go?

That's a bit of a difficult question to answer. First, the US income tax has graduated rates that get higher as one's income rises. Then, there is the difference between the nominal tax rate, which is the theoretical tax rate required by law, and the real tax rate, which is the tax rate that is actually paid after allowable deductions have been included. Someone who makes $250,000 per year is in the highest tax bracket and has a nominal tax rate of 36%. After taking all the allowable deductions—and there are literally thousands in the tax code—that same person will pay a real tax rate of about 22%.

Based on our past experience with tax rates, the equilibrium point is probably somewhere around a real, high tax rate of 25%. Historically, every time high real tax rates have begun to rise above that level, economic activity has started to decline and tax revenues have started to fall. Moreover, when asked directly in opinion polls, Americans have been pretty consistent at picking 25% as the highest fair rate of taxation.

In the past century, there have been four major tax rate reductions. They occurred in 1919, 1946, 1962, and 1981. In all four cases, government revenues rose very sharply after the tax rate cuts, due to robust growth in the economy. As John F. Kennedy said about his tax-cutting plan, "It is paradoxical, but if you want to increase revenues, you must cut tax rates."

There were additional tax rate cuts in the first years of the administration of George W. Bush. Unlike the earlier tax cuts, however the rate reductions were comparatively minor, cutting each tax bracket by a few percent. In contrast, the 1981 Reagan tax cuts slashed all rates at least 15%, and cut the top tax rate from 70% to 33%.

At the time of this writing, we haven't yet seen a strong recovery from the 2001–2002 recession, as we did when earlier tax cuts were made. So, there is an argument that says that tax rates are already hovering close to the Equilibrium Point, so incremental tax cuts don't change the picture significantly.

This argument is strengthened by the experience of the 1990s. Even though the economy was just coming out of a recession after the election of 1992, President Clinton got Congress to make some moderate tax increases. Despite predictions by the Supply-Siders on the Republican side of the debate that these tax increases would cause economic failure, the economy kept expanding. Eventually, the 1990s became the longest period of economic growth since WWII.

Supply-Side Economics

Because of the work of Laffer, and others, most notably economics writer Jude Wanninski, a school of economics called Supply-Side Economics was born in the late 1970s. They key idea behind Supply-Side economics was that tax rates were too high, and needed to be slashed. They used the Laffer Curve as proof of this proposition.

Now, there isn't an economist in the world who doesn't believe that something very much like the Laffer Curve exists. Nor are there too many economists who won't admit that confiscatory tax rates severely hinder economic growth. But knowing those things apparently don't help us much when it comes to the specifics of tax policy and revenue growth.

Notice that the Laffer Curve contains only the most generally defined data points. What is the tax rate at which the equilibrium point is reached? What is the tax rate at Points A or B? The Laffer Curve doesn't tell us.

Indeed, we don't even have any real idea what the equilibrium point is, except to note that it is the highest rate at which the population consents to be taxed. During a major war, the citizenry might be satisfied with the equilibrium point moved quite far to the right, willingly paying high taxes in order to contribute to their national survival. In an era of peace and plenty, the equilibrium point might shift farther to the left.

As a general proposition, of course, tax cuts are a good thing. If nothing else, tax cuts promote economic growth, as people are free to spend more of their money on the goods and services they desire.

But the Supply-Siders' argument went farther than that. They proposed that tax cuts would cause such a large measure of economic growth that revenue for the government would increase substantially.

In the 1970's and early 1980s, with the high marginal tax rates at the time, and high inflation pushing people into higher tax brackets even though their real income was unchanged, it seemed to be a fairly reasonable argument to say that we were at Point B on the Laffer Curve. Almost any tax relief, it was argued, would move us to the left of the curve, and bring us closer to the equilibrium point. While some short-term deficits might result, the Supply-Siders argued, increased revenues would eliminate them in a fairly short time. On this basis, the Reagan tax cuts were implemented.

The end result was that during the Reagan Years (1981–1988) Federal Government receipts increased by only 14.9% (when measured in constant 1996 Dollars to account for inflation). Compare this with the 27.3% revenue growth from 1973–1980, or the 19.8% revenue growth of 1989–1996. Deficits, meanwhile, skyrocketed.

In 1994, I talked weekly on my radio program with Paul Craig Roberts, who was a Deputy Undersecretary of the Treasury in the Reagan administration, and a staunch supply-sider. During this time, while the Clinton Administration pushed for and obtained its tax increases, Roberts would assure me regularly about the dire consequences to come for the economy. Higher taxes, he argued, would stop economic growth, and lead us back into recession.

Instead, between 1993 and 2000, Federal receipts rose from $1.23 trillion to $1.88 trillion (again, in constant 1996 dollars), an increase of 52.3%. There are, it seems, many things other than marginal tax rates that matter when it comes to economic growth.

Between 1981 and 1983 the nation was mired in horrible back-to-back recessions, with double-digit unemployment as the Fed squeezed interest rates higher and higher to combat the inflationary trends of the 1970s. Federal receipts actually declined by 10.6% during those years.

In the 1990s, the information revolution and the huge increases in productivity it engendered more than compensated for any effect the Clinton tax policies might have had. Indeed, while it is true that revenues for the Federal Government grew by 28.4% from 1983–1988, following the recessions of the early 80s, that performance is worse than any six-year period of the Clinton administration. Indeed, in the six years after the Clinton tax increases, revenue grew by 36%. Supply-Siders are fond of blaming the tax increases of President George H.W. Bush for the 1991 recession, but have more difficulty explaining why the Clinton tax increases didn't have the same effect.

Moreover, with marginal tax rates at their current relatively low levels, the Supply-Siders have even more difficulty making the argument that we are still substantially on the right side of the Laffer Curve. If current marginal tax rates are close to the equilibrium point, then further tax reductions move us closer to Point A on the curve, which means revenues will drop, rather than rise. Hence, a real danger exists that further tax cuts will contribute substantially to higher deficits.

So far, that Supply-Side deal hasn't picked up a sterling reputation for accuracy.

Keynesian (Demand-Side) Economics

British economist John Maynard Keynes is easily the most influential economist of this century. His brand of economic thought became almost universally accepted in the west under the name of Keynesianism, or Keynesian Economics. To some extent, almost every developed economy in the world operates along the lines of Keynesian theory.

The classic guide to Keynesian theory—indeed, the culmination of his life's work—is his 1936 book, *The General Theory of Employment, Interest, and Money*. It was in this book that Keynes defined the relationship between fiscal and monetary policy, and their effect on economic growth and employment. As Keynes so ably put it:

$$Y = (1/(1\text{-}MPC\text{+}m))(a - MPC\ NT + I + G + mNT)$$

Yeah. Whatever.

The basis of Keynes' work was to try to find a way to escape the boom and bust gyrations of the business cycle. He thought that the government could do it by the way it spent money. Proving that, however, wasn't easy, because up to that time, Say's Law had been the generally accepted explanation of how the economy worked.

We stated Say's Law in a very simplified form previously, but, in reality, it was a much more profound idea than simply saying, "Supply creates its own demand". What Say was really saying was that the relationship between supply and demand seeks to equalize itself in the economy as a whole. Say thought that if a person made a new product he would try to sell it as quickly as possible in order to buy another product that he wanted. In other words, people produce in order to consume. As such, Say theorized that there could never be a glut of goods in the economy, because people would sell those goods in order to consume others.

Keynes thought differently. Say's law applies, thought Keynes, in a barter economy, where goods have to be traded directly. But once you throw money into the mix, it messes up everything.

A barter economy is fundamentally different than a money-based economy. After all, you can't keep a bushel of apples sitting around forever. They have to be traded or consumed relatively quickly. But, with money, people might not want to spend it immediately. They may wish to save it in order to buy a really nice Pontiac Bonneville, with the heads-up display in the windshield and the 9-position heated, electric driver's seat. They may have to loan it to their worthless brother in law at 5% to prevent their wife from forcing them to sleep on the couch. Money, in short, gives you options for saving and investing that don't exist conveniently in a barter economy.

But that means that people may want to hoard money, rather than spending it. If so, then it is the demand for goods, not their supply, that is the driving force in the economy. If more goods are produced than people are willing to buy, an oversupply of goods is created. "Demand," said Keynes, "creates its own supply." This has been taken by many economists to be a solid disproof of Say's law as it applies to a large economy, although many of Say's insights are still very useful in other circumstances.

Thanks to Keynes, we now know that recessions are caused when people hoard money, or, as economists now say, recessions are "monetary phenomena". What that really means is that people get a hankerin' for hard cold cash, and a recession is caused when there isn't enough of it to go around.

Why would people hoard cash? Well, people like to prepare for the future. One of the ways they do that is by saving money. Maybe someone thinks he's about to lose his job. Or maybe he sees prices starting to rise. So, he thinks, "Maybe I should squirrel away a little extra cash, and maybe I should stop using my credit card and only buy things with cash. And, while I'm at it, maybe I should cut down on my expenses." The end result is that, even though his personal spending might decrease, his demand for cash rises. Unfortunately, once enough people start doing this, cash begins draining out of the economy as the demand for cash begins to rise above its available supply.

When the demand for cash increases and the supply decreases, it doesn't take a rocket scientist to figure out what happens to the price of cash. Now, when we refer to the "price" of cash, we are really referring to the cost of borrowing. Obviously a $20 bill is still worth $20. But, if you need to go to the bank and borrow extra cash, well, they are going to charge you interest on the money you borrow. And, as the amount of available money gets smaller and smaller due to hoarding, the interest rate they charge you will begin to rise, to reflect their decreasing supply of money available for lending.

As the demand for cash rises, this decreases the demand for physical goods. People are less interested in buying things than they are in keeping cash on hand. In addition, rising interest rates make it more expensive to borrow money to expand a business or hire new employees. This causes the economy to slow down, creating a recession.

Keynes thought about all this, and he came up with a solution. What governments really needed to do to avoid recessions, thought Keynes, was to take money away from people who were hoarding it—which, as a practical matter meant wealthier people, since they usually had more cash to spare—and give it to the people who would spend the money, i.e. poorer people, who could always use a new car, or better clothes, or home repairs. To accomplish that, Keynes' idea was to use fiscal and monetary policy to moderate the business cycle.

We'll talk about monetary policy in detail later in this chapter, but as far as fiscal policy goes, Keynes said that in recessions or depressions, the government should use deficit spending to pump more money into the economy. This extra spending would increase the money supply, and stimulate the economy. In addition, government could cut taxes, allowing people to keep more of what they'd earned.

In good economic times, he said the government should operate at a surplus. That would keep the economy from heating up too fast, and set aside a store of money to be spent in the recessionary times. It would also reduce the money supply, and erase the inflationary pressures bought about by increasing the money supply during the recessions. Taxes could also be raised to help make up the previous budget shortfalls.

Keynes' actual theory is, of course, greatly more complex than I've stated it, but those are the essentials.

Keynes' theory is extremely elegant. It is, in fact, almost flawless on paper. When you read it, it all makes perfect sense, and it looks like the perfect way to banish the business cycle once and for all. It only has one, tiny, little error: it requires that politicians administer it.

Keynesian economics has failed.

Politicians just aren't up to administering this kind of system. It is always easy for a politician to vote for an increase in spending, or a cut in taxes. That means more money flows into his home district, so more people are working and making more money, and keeping more of what they earn. Voting to shut that spending down or to raise taxes is far more difficult. That does just the opposite to the politician's district. His voters get angry with him. He loses reelection. In other words, for the system to work, politicians have to vote against their own best interest.

Politicians don't do that.

So, since Keynes' theory became accepted government policy, we've only been doing the easy part. We've increased spending continuously every time the economy has started to slow, but we've never cut back once the recessions were over. So now, we're over seven trillion dollars in debt. That's $7,000,000,000,000.00! That's about $30,000.00 for every single person in the country. So, while Keynes' theories work well on paper, they haven't done very much good in real life, except to get the nations that have used them deeper into debt.

Remember, even communism works on paper.

The fault, of course, is not that of Keynes. The mechanisms he identified have been criticized and modified since 1936, and Say's Law has even started to make a comeback, as economists found that Keynes wasn't as elegantly right as he seemed in 1936. But the economic community generally agrees on the central holdings of his work. It's still used by governments to intervene in the economy, and his observations on how government policies can affect the economy are mainly correct.

So, blame the politicians, not poor John Maynard.

Keynes vs. Supply-Side

But, even if Keynes didn't give us a lasting legacy of sane fiscal policy, what he did give us was a way of connecting the dots between taxation, spending and economic growth.

The Supply-Side theory is an attempt to do the same thing, but it seems to suffer from a serious flaw. At moderate rates of taxation, the predictions of its advocates aren't borne out by experience. It seems that once you've gotten tax rates down to reasonable levels, Supply-Side theory isn't very helpful at predicting the effects of tax cuts or increases on the economy.

Keynesian economics, or, as the modern version of it is known, Neo-Keynesianism, does maintain its predictive power. Instead of concentrating on the supply of money, Keynesian economics concentrates on the demand for money.

Supply-Siders base their economic theory on Say's Law, which we talked about earlier. As you may remember, Say's Law states that supply creates its own demand. In the Supply-Side worldview, by increasing the amount of money available, usually through tax cuts, demand will automatically increase to match the available money supply. So, Supply-Siders believe that having an adequate supply of money drives the economy's demand.

Most economists reject this view. I could show you exactly how economists have disproved Say's Law, but it would require math. Frankly, you don't want to slog through it, and I don't want to write all those prissy little math symbols. The general view however is that Keynes conclusively refuted Say's law, at least as far as it's applied to the economy as a whole.

But we can get a glimpse of how he did it with a thought experiment. I like thought experiments, not only because they don't require any math, but also because they don't require any effort at all, other than gazing blankly into space.

In any event, look at unemployment. Say's law implies that if there is a supply of available workers, there will never be any unemployment because the demand for labor will increase to fully employ the labor supply.

Keynes said that simply can't be right. To assume that, he said, is simply to assume our problems away. Because, after all, we *know* there's unemployment. The standard answer to that was that there was always some amount of unemployment, because people were changing jobs, or temporarily injured. They called this "frictional" unemployment, because it resulted from an economy that wasn't perfectly inefficient. Keynes disproved this idea mathematically.

Then the Great Depression proved it in reality.

Keynes' idea, therefore, was the exact opposite of Say's. Keynes thought that demand was the driving force in the economy. Say's law, instead, was only occasionally applicable, such as explaining how the supply of a new product, like pet rocks, could stimulate a demand that hadn't existed previously.

But, once that demand had been created, it existed independent of the supply. That demand then became the driving economic force. Remember, there isn't any shortage of pet rocks, but I haven't seen any real demand for them, even with our essentially infinite supply.

Yes, pet rocks are an exception to the economic, "everything is scarce" argument.

By focusing on demand, Keynes was able to provide us with a workable and relatively accurate set of economic predictions.

One of the more interesting developments in the 2004 election year was that many well-known Keynesian economists who were also active Democrats criticized the Bush tax cuts for increasing the deficit. One of the central bases of their criticisms was that the tax cuts only helped "the richest" Americans, and did nothing to help average Americans, by bringing back jobs.

This is an odd argument for Keynesians to make. If, in fact, the Keynesian theory holds that lowing taxes and deficit spending help boost the economy, such arguments are counterintuitive, to say the least.

If the problem is that the economy is in recession, and economic growth is needed to spur job growth, then Bush's policies, Republican though they were, would seem to be precisely those policies that Keynes would have recommended.

Perhaps, in some cases, being a good Democrat was more important than being a good Keynesian.

New Tax Policies

There is a raging debate going on now about taxes. There are several proposals on the table to completely overhaul the income tax system we use. The two most popular ideas are the Flat Tax and the National Sales Tax.

Under the Flat Tax proposal, every person in the country would be charged the same tax rate. In most proposals, the tax rate for everybody would be about 19%. Single people would pay that tax rate on all income they make over $18,000.00, a married couple would start paying taxes at $24,000.00, and a family of four would be taxed on income over $36,000.00. And that's it. No other exemption, no other deductions.

For higher income people, the Flat Tax would amount to a tax increase, because they have so many loopholes that their actual tax burden is currently around 22% of their income. For a lot of middle-class Americans, they'd come out even. Lower-income taxpayers might not pay any taxes at all. Additionally, huge savings would be made in time and money because tax returns could be done on a postcard and the vast majority of IRS personnel could be fired. All those accountants and tax lawyers would have to find real jobs, too. This proposal is generating a lot of excitement in Washington.

Tax lawyers and accountants think the whole thing is a terrible idea. IRS workers aren't too thrilled about it either.

The other proposal is the National Sales Tax, or, as the supporters of one version rather self-servingly call it, the "Fair Tax". Under the National Sales Tax (I'll just call it the NST, because I'm lazy and it's shorter.), the personal income tax would be totally eliminated. No more Federal Income Tax withheld from your paycheck. No more IRS at all. No more scrambling to the post office on April 15th. The government would no longer have any business at all asking you nosy personal questions like how much money you made, and what you did with it.

On the other hand, the price of almost everything in the country would rise by 20%.

Obviously, under the NST, poor people would be hit hard, unless a provision was made to exclude staple items like food, clothing, and shelter from the tax. Poor people spend a much larger percentage of their incomes just acquiring these basics.

Taxes that burden lower income earners more than they burden high wage earners are called regressive taxes. Taxes that place a proportionally higher burden on the richer members of society are called progressive taxes. Assuming that the NST would exempt staple items and become more progressive[1], it might be a very effective tax for several reasons.

First, under the income tax code, the rich tend to pay less than their nominal tax rate, because they have the ability to shelter income in ways that many poorer people do not. They also tend to buy many more things, because they have the money to do so. The NST, by taxing consumption instead of income, would not allow them to avoid taxes in the same way the income tax does.

Second, there is a small but significant portion of the population that makes its living in, well, shady ways. Their income is never taxed, because they do not report it. The transactions that are not reported to the government, and incomes derived from those transactions, are said to be the underground economy or black market. The current estimates are that the underground economy is generating income that could be worth hundreds of billions of dollars in revenues. Many of

---

1.   In point of fact, the NST that has been proposed as the "Fair Tax" Does have a fairly extensive list of such exemptions.

these underground transactions are made in cash, though, and are difficult to trace, so it's hard to tell what the actual size of the black market is. But if we assume that the US has a $10 trillion economy, and 10% of that is hidden payments for cocaine and hookers—or doing plumbing or construction work "under the table"—that's an extra $1 trillion floating around out there that would be good for $200 to $300 billion in government revenues.

I want to stress here that I certainly have no personal knowledge whatsoever about any black market dealings of any kind.

The people who work in the underground economy do not pay income tax, but they buy goods and services like the rest of us. Under the NST, those goods and services would be taxed, and revenues would be increased.

Additionally, there is a generally accepted economic rule that says if you tax something, you get less of it. The income tax—and the proposed Flat Tax—taxes production. The NST taxes consumption. If your goal is to reduce consumption and increase savings, while at the same time removing the burden on production, then the NST is probably the best way to do this.

Under the NST, people who get raises or who get new, higher paying jobs actually get to take home that extra money, instead of having it eaten away by being put into a higher income tax bracket. This increases the incentive to earn more by producing more. At the same time, higher prices tend to make people consume less, freeing up more money for savings, which, in turn, can be invested.

The trouble is that there is a debate about what the actual engine of growth is: consumption or production. Demand-side economists believe that it is the demand from consumers that encourage businesses to produce more. Supply-side economists believe that a growth in supply creates demand from consumers, in much the same way that Say's Law says. So, to a large extent, whether someone prefers the NST over the Flat Tax is largely determined by whether they are on the supply or the demand side. The NST tends to be favored by supply-siders. Income taxes like the Flat Tax tend to be favored by demand-siders.

One thing both sides agree on is that the current income tax system is essentially a disaster. It is hugely complicated, and it contains a huge number of loopholes and legal tax avoidance mechanisms. Its complexity makes it almost impossible to understand except to a professionally trained tax lawyer or accountant. This makes their services absolutely indispensable to many businesses and taxpayers.

Actually, it isn't quite correct to say that everybody agrees that the current tax system is a disaster. Tax lawyers and accountants think the current tax code is really great, and IRS workers are absolutely thrilled about it.

In many ways, the current tax system allows the government to rip us off legally. Let's take corporate income taxes. Corporations are taxed at a rate of 33% of their profits every quarter, that is, every three months. Profits that are left over after taxes are distributed to all the shareholders of the company. These distributed profits are called earnings.

If a company has one million shares of stock and makes an after-tax profit of one million dollars, then every shareholder receives one dollar per share as earnings. If you own a thousand shares, then you've just made $1,000.00 in earnings for that quarter. But the government considers that $1,000.00 to be part of your personal income, so you have to pay income tax on it, even though it has already been taxed at the corporation.

In other words, the government taxes one-third of your earnings away from you by taxing it away from the corporation before you even see it. Then when you get what's left, the government taxes one-third of that away from you personally. That's called double taxation. Some people call it robbery, but they are tactless and crude.

Here's another interesting part of the tax code: when you buy a government bond, the government has to pay you back with interest. If you buy a $10,000 30-year treasury bond that pays a 7½% interest rate, the government will pay you $750.00 in interest every year.

Where does the money come from to pay you that interest payment? Taxes. Your taxes. But that interest payment is considered to be taxable income according to the government, so they take about one-third of it back on April 15th. In the end, your actual interest payment is $502.50 every year, meaning that the real interest rate on your bond is about 5%.

It's a pretty neat deal for the government. The government takes $750.00 out of the income tax you pay, and pays it back to you as interest on your bond. Then the government takes back $247.50 for having to go through all that trouble. Some people think that government bonds should be non-taxable, but they're just greedy and unsympathetic to the trouble all this difficult financial stuff causes the government.

Tax Fairness

One of the big political footballs when it comes to tax policy, especially tax cuts, is "fairness". When the Republican Bush Administration began proposing tax cuts in 2001, and making them permanent in 2003–2004, Democratic opponents of the president weren't happy. Democratic National Committee chairman Terry McAuliffe's characterization of the plan was that "Bush chose to reward the wealthiest Americans with a $674 billion tax cut." Citizens for Tax Justice's director, Robert S. McIntyre, said that the plan shows that the president believes "the rich don't have enough money." According to the Democratic Senate Leadership, "the package showers benefits on the wealthiest one percent of Americans." The real problem, according to the Democrats, is that the rich don't pay their "fair share" of taxes.

So, then, just how much of federal income tax revenues do the rich actually pay? According to the IRS, the share of federal taxes paid works out as follows:

Income Level	% of Tax Revenues Paid
Top 1%	37.42
Top 5 %	56.47
Top 10%	67.33
Top 25%	84.01
Top 50%	96.09
Bottom 50%	3.91

Defining who comprises that group called "the rich" is a difficult task, but no matter where you draw the line, it's pretty clear that the rich already pay the lion's share of income taxes. More than 37% of all income tax revenues come from the top 1% of income earners alone. Indeed, the bottom 50% of all taxpayers only contributes 3.9% of all the income tax revenues the government receives.

Much of this disparity is explained by looking at the real income tax rates on people of various income levels. The real tax rate is the amount of their income that people actually pay in taxes, rather than the statutory income brackets set by the IRS. According to "Tax Facts", a joint project of the Urban Institute and the Brookings Institution (neither of which is a particularly right-wing organization, I hasten to point out), the effective income tax rates break down as follows:

Income Level	Effective Tax Rate
Bottom Quintile	-5.3%
Second Quintile	1.3%
Middle Quintile	4.8%
Fourth Quintile	7.5%
Top Quintile	15.8%
Top 10%	17.8%
Top 5%	19.5%
Top 1%	22.3%

The bottom quintile (20%) of income earners actually has a negative income tax. In other words, the income tax actually increases their income by over 5%. At the other end of the scale, a person in the top 1%, making a million dollars a year, actually pays a $223,000 tax bill every April 15th.

By definition, tax cuts benefit taxpayers. If the top 10% is already paying nearly 70% of all income taxes, then logically they will be the people whose taxes are cut the most. It's difficult to cut taxes on, say, the bottom quintile of income earners, who already have a negative effective tax rate. As a practical matter, this means that one can characterize any income tax cut as a benefit to the rich, since they are, in effect, practically the only ones paying it in the first place.

The income tax provides only about half of all federal revenues, yet even at that, the top 10% of taxpayers provide about 30% of the Federal government's total revenue. They pay nearly one-third of the salaries of our soldiers, sailors, and airmen. They provide almost one-third of every highway project, food stamp, Federal courthouse, and welfare check, while the bottom 50% of taxpayers provide less than 4%.

And, remember what happens when you reduce incentives by raising taxes. The more you tax something, i.e., reduce the incentive for doing it by making it more expensive, you get less of it. In the end, excessive taxes on "the rich" are likely to make everyone poorer, as higher taxes reduce the incentive for everyone to achieve.

Just something to keep in mind the next time you hear someone complaining about "tax fairness".

Government Spending

Government spending is the other side of the fiscal policy coin. If the government spends more, that means more money is going to government workers, benefits recipients, or businesses with government contracts. The people who get that extra money will then spend it, and so the effect begins to diffuse itself throughout the economy. If the government spends less, the reverse happens, of course. The thing to remember here is that taxation affects everyone individually, while government spending affects the economy as a whole, and more slowly, by diffusing the extra money through the economy.

Because taxes impact on practically every individual at the same time, tax policy can affect the economy faster than almost any other government act. If the government raised the personal income tax rate to 80% tomorrow, the economy would shut down immediately. People would have to change their lifestyles overnight to accommodate the rise in taxes. That's why taxation has an immediate effect on the economy.

Spending moves more slowly, because the results of spending changes have to filter through the economy as a whole. Look at what happened to the economy in California when defense funding was cut way back in the first part of the 1990s. Defense firms had to lay off thousands of workers. Those workers were then left without jobs and so they had to cut way back on their spending.

With less money being spent by those workers, clothing stores, restaurants, and all sorts of other businesses had less income coming in. That meant more jobs had to be cut at those businesses. With fewer jobs, unemployment rose. The whole state's economy began to grind to a halt. When the economy began to recover in the rest of the country, California's recovery was much slower, because there was more inertia to overcome. So, the next time you start raving about how the government should cut spending, just remember that spending cuts will slow down the economy to some degree.

Politicians have known this for years, of course. That's why it's always easier for politicians to increase spending than to cut it. If a congressman increases the amount of Federal money coming into his district, he's a hero to the folks at home.

That's why West Virginia has, thanks to their long-time Senator Robert Byrd (D), everything from the Robert Byrd Highway Overpass to the Robert Byrd Water Treatment Plant to the Robert Byrd Empty Field Where Something Grandiose Will Be Built In Appreciation of

Robert Byrd. That's also why he's been that state's senior senator since the earth cooled.

When a politician is Byrd-like in his ability to bring that Federal Pork home, there are more jobs and money to go around for his constituents. But if that same politician cuts spending in his home district, then some people are going to lose jobs. That will make the voters unhappy. Unhappy voters don't re-elect politicians. Do the math.

It's difficult to run a sane fiscal policy when the easiest votes to get a politician to cast are votes for tax cuts and spending increases.

At this point you're probably asking, "Well, if cutting taxes and increasing government spending both stimulate the economy, then why not just do it and let the economy just go on a tear?" Okay, fair question. Let me ask one in return. Why don't you quit your job tomorrow and live off your Visa, MasterCard, and American Express card?

You see, if an economic policy won't work in your personal life, it probably won't work as a macroeconomic policy for the whole country either. At some point, the credit card companies aren't going to let you have any more money. And they'll want the money they've already given you back. Sure, for a while you can appear to be very well off. You can buy all sorts of neat stuff. But when the bills are due and you can't pay, the party's over. The same thing happens to the government.

From 1980 to 1996, government revenues rose continuously. The government was taking in more money than it ever had before. At the same time, the government spent nearly four trillion dollars more than it took in from taxes. For most of that time the country was very prosperous. But, as Senator Lloyd Bentsen quipped during the 1988 election campaign, "If I could write four hundred billion dollars in bad checks every year, I'd look prosperous, too."

How the federal government spends money can directly affect the way you and I live. Government spending can create growth in different sectors of the economy. Let's say the politicians all decide that people in the state of Maine are too poor. The federal government could start massive public works projects in the state, and pump billions of dollars into the Maine. Jobs would be created. People might flock to Maine to get one of those jobs. More money would be thrown into the state's economy as the workers began to spend their paychecks. Since the residents would all have jobs, entertainment services would begin to thrive. Restaurants would open up. Theaters and bars would pop up everywhere. Before you know it, everybody in Maine would be employed, well-fed, entertained, and intoxicated.

But you have to remember, that while the folks in Maine would enjoy it, the money used to create all that growth would come out of the pockets of all the taxpayers all over the country who don't live in Maine. All the rest of us would have less money and, presumably, less fun.

The thing to remember is that, since the government produces nothing, it can only shift money around from one group of taxpayers to another. The government is then said to transfer wealth from one sector of the economy to another. In this sense, fiscal policy is a zero-sum game.

At the end of the Cold War, the government began to make massive cutbacks in the military. The money that would be saved by these cutbacks was referred to as the "peace dividend". Defense spending fell sharply. The government was supposed to be able to simply cut that spending out and perhaps cut everybody's taxes to compensate for the decreased spending.

What actually happened was that the government just spent that money on other things. But for hundreds of thousands of military personnel, defense workers, and Defense Department civilians it meant they were out of a job. Military bases were closed. The communities that surrounded those military bases lost billions of dollars in spending in their local economies. In fact, the state of California, where many defense contractors had their factories and where many military bases were located, went into a severe recession, with high unemployment, great numbers of business failures, and commensurably higher social spending for things like unemployment payments. Californians didn't consider peace to be such a dividend.

The point to all of this is that government spending can have a huge effect throughout the economy. If the government decides to spend money in a certain sector of the economy, then that sector will probably thrive. But by the same token, decreases in government spending may cause quite a lot of economic pain, even if the long-term effect is positive.

Government spends a lot of money. The tables below show government spending over several recent years. Each chart gives you a slightly different view of the same spending data.

Government Spending By Agency, 2000–2003
(In millions of dollars)

Department or other unit	2000	2001	2002	2003
Legislative Branch	2,911	3,034	3,218	3,427
The Judiciary	4,086	4,405	4,823	5,123
Agriculture	75,487	67,951	68,731	72,390
Commerce	7,803	5,010	5,314	5,676
Defense—Military	281,161	290,960	331,951	388,870
Education	33,900	35,721	46,282	57,400
Energy	14,982	16,340	17,681	19,385
Health and Human Services	382,552	426,311	465,812	505,345
Homeland Security	13,134	15,025	17,557	31,967
Housing and Urban Development	30,828	33,939	31,885	37,474
Interior	8,029	7,868	9,739	9,210
Justice	17,254	18,695	21,112	21,539
Labor	31,876	39,755	64,704	69,593
State	6,850	7,444	9,453	9,261
Transportation	41,499	49,282	56,024	50,807
Treasury	388,559	386,906	370,558	366,987
Veterans Affairs	47,087	45,050	50,884	56,887
Corps of Engineers	4,333	4,726	4,797	4,751
Other Defense—Civil Programs	32,864	34,164	35,157	39,883
Environmental Protection Agency	7,238	7,391	7,450	8,061
Executive Office of the President	283	246	451	387
General Services Administration	-226	-275	-677	573
International Assistance Programs	12,093	11,777	13,336	13,462
National Aeronautics and Space Administration	13,442	14,095	14,430	14,552
National Science Foundation	3,487	3,690	4,188	4,736
Office of Personnel Management	48,660	50,914	52,512	54,136
Small Business Administration	-421	-570	493	1,558
Social Security Administration (On-budget)	45,121	40,007	45,816	46,333
Social Security Administration (Off-budget)	396,169	421,257	442,011	461,401
Other Independent Agencies (On-budget)	8,722	11,475	16,636	12,158
Other Independent Agencies (Off-budget)	2,029	2,302	-651	-5,245
Allowances	....	....	....	....
Undistributed offsetting receipts	-173,019	-191,125	-200,707	-210,450
(On-budget)	-105,586	-114,404	-115,009	-117,303
(Off-budget)	-67,433	-76,721	-85,698	-93,147
Total outlays	**1,788,773**	**1,863,770**	**2,010,970**	**2,157,637**

Government Spending By Function, 2000–2003
(In millions of dollars)

Superfunction and Function	2000	2001	2002	2003
National defense	294,495	305,500	348,555	404,920
Human resources	1,115,481	1,194,409	1,317,437	1,417,707
Education, training, employment, and social services	53,754	57,143	70,544	82,568
Health	154,533	172,270	196,544	219,576
Medicare	197,113	217,384	230,855	249,433
Income security	253,575	269,615	312,530	334,432
Social security	409,423	432,958	455,980	474,680
(On-budget)	13,254	11,701	13,969	13,279
(Off-budget)	396,169	421,257	442,011	461,401
Veterans benefits and services	47,083	45,039	50,984	57,018
Physical resources	84,653	97,759	104,359	113,240
Energy	-1,061	38	482	-775
Natural resources and environment	25,031	25,623	29,454	29,703
Commerce and housing credit	3,207	5,878	-391	-1,607
(On-budget)	1,178	3,576	260	3,638
(Off-budget)	2,029	2,302	-651	-5,245
Transportation	46,853	54,447	61,833	67,069
Community and regional development	10,623	11,773	12,981	18,850
Net interest	222,951	206,168	170,951	153,076
(On-budget)	282,747	274,979	247,771	236,621
(Off-budget)	-59,796	-68,811	-76,820	-83,545
Other functions	113,774	106,945	117,060	123,076
International affairs	17,216	16,493	22,351	21,208
General science, space and technology	18,633	19,784	20,767	20,873
Agriculture	36,465	26,204	21,957	22,600
Administration of justice	28,501	30,205	35,171	35,408
General government	12,959	14,259	16,814	22,987
Allowances	....	....	....	....
Undistributed offsetting receipts	-42,581	-47,011	-47,392	-54,382
(On-budget)	-34,944	-39,101	-38,514	-44,780
(Off-budget)	-7,637	-7,910	-8,878	-9,602
Total, Federal outlays	1,788,773	1,863,770	2,010,970	2,157,637
(On-budget)	1,458,008	1,516,932	1,655,308	1,794,628
(Off-budget)	330,765	346,838	355,662	363,009

Government Spending As Percentages of Outlays, 2000–2003

Function	2000	2001	2002	2003
National defense	16.5	16.4	17.3	18.8
Human resources	62.4	64.1	65.5	65.7
Physical resources	4.7	5.2	5.2	5.2
Net interest	12.5	11.1	8.5	7.1
Other functions	6.4	5.7	5.8	5.7
Undistributed offsetting receipts	-2.4	-2.5	-2.4	-2.5
Total, Federal outlays	**100.0**	**100.0**	**100.0**	**100.0**
(On-budget)	81.5	81.4	82.3	83.2
(Off-budget)	18.5	18.6	17.7	16.8

Government Spending As Percentages of GDP, 2000–2003

Function	2000	2001	2002	2003
National defense	3.0	3.0	3.4	3.7
Human resources	11.5	11.9	12.7	13.1
Physical resources	0.9	1.0	1.0	1.0
Net interest	2.3	2.1	1.6	1.4
Other functions	1.2	1.1	1.1	1.1
Undistributed offsetting receipts	-0.4	-0.5	-0.5	-0.5
Total, Federal outlays	**18.4**	**18.6**	**19.4**	**19.9**
(On-budget)	15.0	15.1	16.0	16.6
(Off-budget)	3.4	3.5	3.4	3.4

The Federal Budget

So far we've only looked at the spending side of the federal government. The budget, however, includes both the revenues the government takes in, and the outlays it spends on various programs.

The budget the federal government uses is a lot like yours, but with a lot more zeros at the ends of all the numbers.

Until recently, the government used a budgeting method called the Current Services Baseline. Each year, the congress would take a look at what was spent in the previous year. Then, they would just assume an increase of X percent should take place in spending, and add it to that budget item. That new amount would be the baseline budget.

Now, that's different than what you and I use to balance our budgets. When we do our own budgets, we use a method called zero-based budgeting. With zero-based budgeting, you start off assuming your checking account is empty until you deposit money in it. You then write checks, and deduct money from your account until you get back down to zero. When you hit zero, you know that if you write any more checks, you'll get to take a ride in one of those nice new Ford Crown Victorias the Sheriff's Department just bought.

With the current services baseline, the government doesn't start off by saying, "Okay, how much money are we going to take in this year?" Instead, it starts off by saying, "Here is how much we're gonna spend". If they don't take in enough money in taxes, they just borrow the difference. Deciding how much money is going to be spent is done without any reference to how much money the government will take in through taxation.

This type of budgeting treats projected baseline spending increases as if they were really necessary, without taking into account whether or not the money actually needs to be spent. For example, the baseline spending increase for Medicare has been set around 11% per year for the last few years. Were there 11% more recipients each year? No. Did prices for medical services rise by 11% each year? No. But that's how much spending increased because the baseline said so. For many budget items, the increases in baseline spending are mandated by law, and cannot be changed unless Congress changes the law, and the president signs the change into a new law.

The Republican plan for balancing the budget, which was presented in congress in 1995, called for 5% increases in Medicare spending, instead of the 11% that was included in the baseline projections. Democrats said that amounted to a huge cut in spending. They said hundreds of millions of dollars would be taken away from elderly people. But that's a bit disingenuous. Per capita spending for each Medicare recipient actually increased under the Republican plan. But because current services baseline treats the spending projection as if it were real money, Democrats called those spending increases a "cut" in spending, because the Republican increase in spending was less than the 11% projected in the baseline, even though the amount of money being spent was increasing in real terms by 5%.

Let's apply it to real life. Let's say you make $30,000.00 a year, and you work at a company that regularly gives 10% pay increases every year. (By the way, I'd like the number of the personnel department for that company. It sounds like a place where I'd like to work.) But company management announces that, starting next year, raises in pay will now be limited to 5% each year. Would you resign because your salary was going to be cut by 50% over the next ten years? Of course, not! Even assuming you never got promoted to a higher paying position, those 5% salary increases would mean that at the end of ten years, you'd be making about $49,000. But in the world of current services baseline budgeting, that's called a spending cut.

Just like your salary in the previous example, the only thing the Republicans cut from Medicare was the rate of growth. Current services baseline allows for a lot of free political rhetoric, so politicians find it useful. It allows politicians to pretend that the baseline spending projections are what really must be spent, and that problems with the deficit don't come from too much spending, but too little revenue. But those baseline projections are only arbitrary levels of spending. Baseline budgeting doesn't allow for changes that make higher spending levels unnecessary. It also makes budget cutting harder, because any reduction in the rate of spending increase is decried as a cut.

Just remember, if you tried to do your personal finances using the current services baseline, you'd get to personally know all of the sheriff's deputies in your county, and the exact performance specifications of every Crown Vic in the county fleet.

The Republican-led congress changed to zero-based budgeting in 1995 as part of the "Contract with America." Changing to zero-based budgeting makes government spending a little more comprehensible to the average person. With zero-based budgeting, the baseline spending increases are eliminated. Each year, Congress starts off assuming that spending this year will be exactly the same as spending last year. Then they decide whether to increase or decrease spending in each area of the budget. If spending in a particular area increases, it's called an increase.

One of the biggest debates about the budget is how to balance it, and keep it balanced. The Federal Government had a balanced budget in 1998 and 1999. In fact, it even ended up with a surplus for those years, which means the government spent less money than it took in through revenues. This was the first time the budget had been balanced since 1968. Surpluses in the Federal Budget were predicted for the next several years.

But did those surpluses actually materialize?

Uh, no.

The economy began to slow in the second half of 2000, and by the first quarter of 2001, we had slipped into a recession. As a result, government revenues were much lower than had been projected just two years earlier.

Then on September 11th, 2001, the horrific terrorist attacks on the World Trade Centers in New York, and the Pentagon in Washington, DC, occurred. In addition to the more than 3,000 deaths in the attacks, tens of thousands of people instantly lost their jobs. Within 60 days, several hundred thousand of people lost their jobs.

The 9/11 attacks were a terrible shock to the economy. For months, airline travel fell to almost nothing. Hundreds of thousands of people in New York were without offices or homes, and many of them without jobs. The ripples of 9/11 were felt throughout the country's economy over the weeks and months after the attacks. What had been a relatively mild recession was significantly deepened by 9/11.

At the same time, the government's response to the attacks required greatly increased spending. Spending on homeland security skyrocketed, as well as military spending for the war against the Taliban in Afghanistan, and the regime of Saddam Hussein in Iraq.

At the same time, the Bush Administration asked for, and Congress passed a series of tax cuts. Those tax cuts reduced federal revenues even more.

In 2001, the federal budget had a surplus of $127.4 billion. In 2002, the budget ran a deficit of-$157.8 billion. In 2003, the deficit was-$375.3 billion. All of the projections for years' worth of budget surpluses disappeared.

According to the Congressional Budget Office (CBO), there were three contributing factors to the new budget deficits. The CBO estimated that revenue losses from the tax cuts were responsible for 36% of the budget deficit. Increases in homeland security and military spending accounted for an additional 31%. The remaining 53% was due to the loss of revenues due to the economic slowdown that started in the first months of 2001.

This highlights one of the difficulties of creating a budget for the Federal government. Most of us have a steady source of income, and a relatively steady amount of debts or bills. That allows us to budget our money based on known figures. The federal government, on the other hand is subject to massive changes in revenues due to outside events, such as the recession or the 9/11 attacks.

Government can set tax rates and control spending, which offsets some of this risk. But much of the government's budget is affected by events entirely outside of its control.

What makes it even worse is that a majority of the federal government's spending is mandatory. The spending amounts are essentially part of the law, and the money must be spent. In the 2003 budget, which totaled $2.16 trillion, mandatory spending totaled $1.33 trillion. This left only $826 billion of the budget for discretionary spending. Simply put, much of the federal government's spending is beyond its control, unless Congress acts to change the laws that require this mandatory spending.

We've already seen the tables that show us federal spending, so let's take a look at the federal government's revenues for the same period.

Federal Government Revenues, 2000–2003
(In millions of dollars)

Source	2000	2001	2002	2003
Individual Income Taxes	1,004,462	994,339	858,345	793,699
Corporate Income Taxes	207,289	151,075	148,044	131,778
Social Insurance and Retirement Receipts	652,852	693,967	700,760	712,978
Excise Taxes	68,865	66,232	66,989	67,524
Other	91,750	85,581	79,035	76,363
Total	**2,025,218**	**1,991,194**	**1,853,173**	**1,782,342**

As you can see, while federal spending has continued to climb, federal revenues have continued to decline. That's a bad thing. Obviously, you can't keep spending more money than you take in forever. So where do you start to cut?

First of all, you look at the discretionary spending. Discretionary spending can be cut easily, because there's no law concerning how much has to be spent in any given area. But all of the discretionary spending put together only accounts for about 38% of the budget. And, frankly, most of what can be cut already has, or it's been transferred into homeland security and military spending due to the War on Terror. So, you're not going to get a lot of mileage out of discretionary cuts.

There are a lot of people who think that cutting off aid to the heathen foreigners would go a long way towards balancing the budget.

Wrong. All foreign aid comes out of the State Department's budget, which comes under the heading of International Affairs. That's 1.4% of the whole budget. The proportion of the federal budget that goes towards foreign aid is about the same as the proportion of your income that you spend on hats.

That leaves the mandatory programs. They are tougher to cut, because the amount spent on mandatory programs is required by federal law. It takes an act of congress to change that spending. And the three areas where most savings can be gleaned are almost politically untouchable, except at the edges: Social security, Medicare, and Medicaid. Without touching those areas, it's almost impossible to balance the budget, or to keep it balanced.

The Congress and President Clinton, in the face of fairly strong opposition, managed to work out a Medicare reform bill and pass it into law. This bill reduced the amount of spending increases in Medicare over the next several years. With this, and other compromises, the budget was finally put into balance in 1998. But they had the help of a strong economy that increased government revenues through taxes, while they trimmed spending increases. If there had been a recession in 1998, there would have been no balanced budget.

In the time since, economic and political events have pushed us back into deficit. Additionally, President Bush and Congress worked out a new Prescription Drug Benefit for Medicare. The price tag for that new benefit now adds another federal spending program to the law, which essentially reverses the Medicare reform enacted during the Clinton Administration.

Cutting mandatory spending is evidently a lot harder than it looks.

But, since 2003, the economy has started to grow again. Does the picture I've painted so far make the future look equally as bleak?

Fortunately, no. You see, the economy isn't static. It generally grows every year, except for periods of recession. In 1992–1999, the economy grew by 3%–4% per year. That means that there was 4% more money being made, and at least 4% more revenue for the government. As the economy grows, so does revenue for the federal government, because the tax base is expanding.

Theoretically, as long as the economy is growing, if the government just froze spending at current levels, the deficit would decrease, because revenues would rise at approximately the same pace as GDP growth.

Of course, if you absolutely freeze spending, that would amount to a budget cut over time. For example, if you freeze Medicare spending, but the number of persons eligible for it increases, that amounts to a reduction in spending per person.

But you don't have to freeze spending at current levels. All you have to do is increase spending at a rate slightly less than GDP growth, and everything will eventually balance out. It will take longer, but eventually the budget will have enough of a surplus to increase spending in times of need without throwing it out of balance again.

We hope.

The real question is, do we really *need* to balance the budget every year?

No. In the current War on Terror, we certainly want the government to be able to borrow as much money as it needs to insure that the required number of foreigners got killed. And there are other situations where a little borrowing might be prudent.

Let's say we wanted to completely revamp the county's transportation system. Over the long term, a major improvement in infrastructure might pay off quite handsomely by making our national transportation system more efficient. But initially, we'd have to borrow the money to do it. And there are lots of other situations where the ability for the government to borrow money comes in handy.

In fact, the government can borrow quite a lot of money for quite a long time with no disastrous effect. But the borrowing has to be done wisely, just like your own borrowing has to be done wisely. The federal government isn't in serious trouble with borrowing yet. We're not having any great crisis. The government only spends 7.1% of its revenues to service the national debt. If you have a car, a mortgage and a credit card, you're probably spending a lot more than 7.1% of your income to service your debts.

The problem isn't the amount of money we owe, the problem is that for most of the last three decades, we've kept borrowing and borrowing and borrowing. If we don't reverse that trend, we will be in trouble in the future. All this cool government swag we're getting isn't free. And someday, it's all gonna have to be paid for.

As a general rule, of course, the less borrowing the government does the better. Remember, every time the government borrows, it does so by selling bonds. If the government sells $200 billion in bonds every year, that is $200 billion that is not going into investment into other sectors of the economy. Most economists believe that government bonds crowd out other forms of investment. Since the government produces nothing, that means there is less investment money for the part of the economy that creates wealth. We'll talk about this in further detail when we discuss the bond market in the next chapter.

Regulation

Regulation is another important power of government. Compliance with federal, state, and local regulations costs businesses millions and millions of dollars a year. Some regulations are more trouble than they're worth. But they all have to be complied with. Regulations are usually written in order to provide guidelines for complying with a law.

When congress passes a law, the language of the law is usually pretty vague. Let's say congress wants to pass the Employee Coffee Break and Snack Act of 2004. Congress will say something like, "All employers shall provide tasty snacks to their employees during break periods." That's it. That becomes the law. But what kind of snacks should be provided? If you give a single Twinkie to each employee, can that count as their snack, or do you have to give them two? If one of your employees is a vegetarian, do you have to provide fresh produce? The law doesn't say. That's where regulation comes in.

Once congress passes the Employee Coffee Break and Snack Act, bureaucrats will descend from the Labor Department like a horde of locusts. They will write down precisely what constitutes a snack, how many calories a snack must contain, how often snacks must be served, whether or not a soft drink can be substituted for coffee during snacks, and a whole host of other issues. The legislation may be one or two pages long, but the Labor Department will issue a 300-page manual of regulations for implementing the act. It sounds silly, but that's what the cabinet departments do. It's how they justify their budgets.

If the regulations say a single Twinkie constitutes a snack, employers will get off relatively cheaply. If the Labor Department says that all employers must provide a choice of sweets, garden-fresh vegetables, beef jerky, and imported caviar on little wheat crackers with cream cheese, snack time at the office is gonna get expensive.

The regulations put out by the government are not laws. But if you break them, you'll go to jail or be fined anyway. Because they implement a federal law, they take on the force of law, even though the regulations are nowhere mentioned in the actual legislation. That gives bureaucrats a lot of power, even though they are not elected, and don't answer directly to the public.

Not all regulations are bad, of course. There are regulations that say businesses can't store toxic waste around unprotected employees. That's a good regulation. But some regulations are silly.

My grandfather was a contractor, and he used to build some large buildings. On one large job, workers were high up on scaffolding. Federal safety regulations required that the scaffolds all have safety bars around the edges so no one could fall off. Unfortunately, at one point during the construction, the safety rails were at exactly the height of the area where work needed to be done.

If the rails were removed on the side of the scaffolding where the building was, the workers could do the work, and they couldn't fall because the building was there. If the rails remained on that side, the work couldn't be done. A safety inspector from the federal Occupational Safety and Health Administration came on site and ordered that the rails be put back on the scaffolding. My grandfather tried to explain the problem to him. They showed him that it would be impossible to fall off of the scaffolding on that side. They showed him that work on the building would never be finished unless the railing came off on the side next to the building. He didn't care. He wanted the regulation strictly enforced. For the next few days, every time the safety inspector came by, the safety rails were put back on and all work stopped until he left.

The regulation was a good one overall. After all, no one wants workers to be taking accidental swan dives off of 50-foot scaffolds. But sometimes you can take a good thing too far. In this case, the regulator held up construction for nearly two whole days, just so that the site would be in compliance when he came by.

Magnify that by every regulation in the books, enforced on every business in the country, and you can see that regulation adds a lot to the cost of doing business.

One of the most outstanding examples of regulation gone haywire was the now defunct zero-emissions mandate that the states of California, Massachusetts, and New York placed on the major auto manufacturers in 1995. At the time, those states decided that in 1998, 2% of the cars in that the auto makers offered for sale in those states must emit no pollutants whatsoever. By the year 2007, 10% of all cars offered for sale were to be zero-emissions vehicles. If the automakers did not produce those vehicles and offer them for sale in those states, they will be banned from doing any business at all.

Legislators gave several environmental reasons for supporting such a mandate. First, they said, it starts with coverage of only 2% of the cars the auto makers sell. Besides, it makes the air cleaner, and helps clean up the horrible smog problems in LA and Boston. It also conserves fuel, and provides an incentive to conservation by vehicle owners. And without a legal requirement, the auto makers simply wouldn't do it. The car makers have resisted every attempt at environmental and safety regulation since seat belts. Therefore the mandate is required to force car makers to help clean up the air. Without it they will probably do nothing.

But let's look at this from a purely economic point of view, and try to see how easy it would be for the car makers to sell these vehicles. Let's take GM. According to the mandate, they were required to offer 30,000 zero-emissions vehicles for sale in California in 2007.

The only technology currently available that emits no pollution is electric technology. The only batteries currently in use that can be mass-produced for the type of power load these electric cars will need is the good old lead-acid battery and a new type of battery called the Nickel-Metal Hydride Battery.

GM has had an electric vehicle research division for decades, and this is the best they've got after 30 years of research. Oh, sure, they're fooling around with hydrogen power cells, and solar energy, and fly-wheels, and a host of other stuff. But batteries of one type or another are essentially it as far as technology that is ready to go off the shelf, as it were.

That means that General Motors was going to have to design—and in fact, they eventually produced—an electric vehicle powered by lead-acid batteries. It was called the EV1. Much like the zero-emissions mandate, the EV1 is now defunct, too.

Notice also that the word "defunct" keeps cropping up in relation to this regulatory boondoggle.

First the car had to be designed and produced. Since no one had ever made an electric car before, that meant a vehicle had to be designed from scratch. With the exception of body shape, an electric car has very little in common with a gasoline-powered vehicle, so it can't be produced on a regular assembly line.

That means a new assembly line had to be designed and built, too. So, before the first car rolled off the assembly line, GM had to spend several million dollars just getting ready to produce the first EV1. Because this is a totally new type of vehicle, entirely new production machines had to be built, so the company couldn't even save money by using existing engine assembly lines, or drive train assembly equipment. Everything had to be brand new.

Then, GM had to figure out how much to sell the car for. And this is where the hard cold bottom line starts to make electric cars look less attractive.

Let me sidetrack for a minute. Let's say you want to make a new widget. Now you have to set up a factory to make these widgets. Let's say it costs a million dollars to build your new widget factory, buy the materials, and hire the labor to make widgets.

The price you charge for your widgets is going to depend in large part on how many widgets you make. If you only make one widget, you're going to have to sell it for one million dollars, just to break even. If you make a million widgets, you can sell them for one dollar apiece. But to avoid losing money on your widget-making business, you have to recover that million-dollar expense for building the factory, or you have to shut the doors and go home.

Now, back to GM. The company spent about $300 million in designing the cars and production facilities. To get that 300 mil back, GM had to price the car at about $30,000.00 just to break even on they price they get from dealers. But the dealer is going to want to make some money on the car, so add about 10% and you come up with the price you'll pay in the showroom. GM's Manufacturer Suggested Retail Price was $33,995.00 for the EV-1 with the lead-acid batteries, and $43,995.00 for the Nickel-Metal Hydride version.

Let's say you bought the cheaper version with the lead-acid batteries. Let's take a look at what your 34 grand got you: An electric vehicle has a maximum range of about 100 miles between recharges. That is assuming optimum driving conditions on a level surface, without using the radio, air conditioning, windshield wipers, headlights, or any other electric device in the car. A recharge takes about 8 hours. Every three years or so, the power of lead-acid batteries runs down, so all 27 batteries have to be replaced. That costs about $3,000.00. The maximum speed of the vehicle was around 60 miles per hour. And there were very few places to charge these cars outside the home, meaning that you really couldn't go very far away from home.

Would you pay $33.995.00 for this car? Remember the cool Pontiac Bonneville we talked about in chapter one? If I was buying a GM product, and was going to spend that kind of money, I'd buy the Bonneville.

There were a lot of people inside and outside the auto business who thought those electric cars were just going to gather dust in the showrooms until the car companies could both improve performance and bring the price way down.

By the way, what would have happened to GM if nobody wanted to buy the car? Or if GM didn't sell all 6,000 cars it was supposed to offer in 1998? Under the mandate, GM would have had to suck up its losses and put another 9,000 electric cars on showroom floors in 1999. By 2007, GM was supposed to have 30,000 electric cars available for sale whether people wanted them or not.

Or, they could decide not to offer any of their products to the 43 million residents of California.

The car manufacturers tried to put a good face on it. I talked to Chrysler's head of zero emissions cars in 1995. He told me that Chrysler would do what it had to under the law. If Chrysler had to sell the cars, it would sell them. Chrysler sales people were the best in the world, he assured me. After all, they sold the K-Car for five years, didn't they?

Well, good point.

In the end, though, the zero-emissions mandate failed. In the real world, all the laws and regulations in the world can't force a technology into existence if the science isn't there. So the mandate died a quiet death.

GM was still out 300 million bucks, though, weren't they? One wonders what productive use that money could have been put to without trying to conform to an impossible regulatory mandate.

The Deficit and the National Debt

People tend to get the deficit and the national debt confused. I will now unconfuse the two terms. Stay with me here.

Let's say that in a single year, the government takes in $1.5 trillion dollars in revenue. If the government spends only $1.3 trillion, then the government has a surplus of $0.2 trillion. But if the government spends $1.7 trillion, it then has a shortfall of $0.2 trillion. That shortfall, or deficit, is that amount of money the government spends over its revenue. In other words, the deficit is the amount of money the government has to borrow in a single year.

The national debt is how much money the government owes from all of the borrowing it has ever done since 1776.

As we've seen, in 2003, the deficit was $375.3 billion. By the end of the year, the total national debt was $6.8 trillion.

So, who does the government borrow all this money from? When the government needs to borrow money, the president doesn't just walk down to First National Bank and start filling out loan paperwork. The government issues bonds.

A bond is a promissory note the government sells through the Department of the Treasury. When you buy a bond, you are loaning money to the government for a certain amount of time. In return, the government promises to pay all of your money back to you, with a reasonably attractive rate of interest, in the time specified. When the government pays you back all your money, plus interest, the bond is then said to have matured. On, the other hand, if the government can't pay off that bond, it is said to be in default.

You can buy a bond that matures in as little as one year, or you can buy a bond that matures in thirty years. US Treasury Bonds come in a variety of maturity lengths: one year, two years, three years, five years, seven years, ten years, and thirty years.

The interest rate that the government pays you back varies, but in general, the longer the maturity on the bond, the higher the interest rate. The thirty-year bond historically pays about 7.5%. The two year bond pays about 6.25%. But these figures will vary quite a bit.

Bonds are also unsecured. That means the government is borrowing the money from you, without promising to give you anything in return if they can't pay you back. But they are backed by the full faith and credit of the United States Government and the government can just print the money up when the time comes to pay you off, so they are considered a risk-free investment. But since they're unsecured, you can't go to the nearest air force base and repossess a fighter plane if they don't pay you back.

Basically, when the government buys a bond, they are saying to you, "Hey, can I borrow ten grand for a few years? I'll pay you back. Really. I'm good for it." This is lot like how you borrow money from your family. Except that you can't just print up the money to pay your family back, like the government does.

Well, you could, but the government takes a dim view of that.

I'll explain bonds more fully in a later chapter.

MONETARY POLICY

Monetary policy is how the government regulates the supply of the currency. It's an important job, because if there is too much money in the economy, the value of the dollar will fall, which means prices will rise. If there is too little money in the economy, the dollar's value will rise, which can put the economy into recession.

The Federal Reserve System

The government body responsible for regulating the money supply is called the central bank. In simple terms, a nation's central bank is where banks go for their banking needs. In Germany, the central bank is the Deutsche Bundesbank; or German Federal Bank. In The United

Kingdom, the central bank is the Bank of England. Here in the US, the central bank is the Federal Reserve System, or the Fed.

Most countries only have one central bank, but in the US, The Federal Reserve System is made up of twelve regional banks, which have twenty-five branches throughout the country. Every nationally chartered bank is required to be part of the Federal Reserve System. Some state-chartered banks can also join the Fed, if they can meet certain requirements.

Governing this whole system are the seven members of the Board of Governors. The president appoints these Governors, and the Senate ratifies the appointments. Governors serve fourteen-year terms. One Governor is selected by the president to serve a four-year term as Chairman of the Board of Governors of the Federal Reserve (a slightly more impressive title than Frank Sinatra's, who was, after all, only Chairman of the Board).

Below them are the twelve Federal Reserve Banks. A nine-member board rules those banks as well. The banks choose six members of the board, three of which must be non-bankers. The other three are chosen by the Fed Governors. One of the board members chosen by the bank becomes president of that Federal Reserve Bank. (There has got to be a simpler way to do this.)

All of the paper money in the country comes out of the Fed. Reach into your pocket and take out a bill. If it is one of the post-1998 currency notes, then on the face side of the bill, there is a black seal to the left of the picture. Around the edge of the seal, you'll see the words "United States Federal Reserve System". The Fed controls how many of these bills are floating around at any given time.

The actual control of monetary policy rests with a body called the Federal Reserve's Federal Open Markets Committee, or FOMC. The FOMC consists of twelve officials of the Federal Reserve: The seven-member Board of Governors, and the presidents of five of the nation's Federal Reserve Banks. The bank presidents are periodically rotated so that all twelve of them eventually get a turn on the FOMC at one time or another.

The Monetary Toolbox

The FOMC controls monetary policy in three ways: changing reserve requirements, changing the discount rate, and open-market operations. Let's talk about these one at a time.

First, the Fed can change reserve requirements of its member banks. Each member bank is required to keep a certain amount of cash on hand, or in reserve. This is usually a set percentage of the bank's total assets. By raising reserve requirements, the Fed forces banks to slow down lending, in order to keep more cash on hand, thus decreasing the money supply. If the Fed lowers reserve requirements, the opposite happens.

As a general practice, the Fed doesn't monkey around too much with reserve requirements, because doing so makes it difficult for banks to do business planning. In practice, the fed has usually let this monetary tool just sit in the toolbox.

The discount rate is the interest rate the Fed charges all member banks to borrow money from the Fed system. If the rate is raised, that makes it more expensive for the bank to borrow money. That means the bank must charge higher interest rates to its customers. The extra money bought in to the Fed by raising the discount rate is, in effect, taken out of the economy. That contracts the supply of money. This is the only interest rate directly controlled by the Fed.

This is actually a pretty effective tool of monetary policy, and it is the one the Fed uses most often.

It's difficult for a bank to know exactly how much of its assets are in cash at any given time during the day. After the bank closes, it does its internal accounting, and settles the books. If it finds that it doesn't have enough money to meet the reserve requirement, the bank has to borrow money overnight from the Fed. This borrowing is charged at the discount rate.

Open-market operations are the buying and selling of securities—mainly bonds—by the Fed, in what is called the Fed Funds market. When the Fed buys securities from member banks, they pay with Federal Reserve Checks, which puts money back into the economy and increases the money supply. If the Fed sells securities to its member banks, the money it makes from those banks is effectively taken out of the economy. Use of this tool affects not only the banks that are members of the Fed system, but every bank that buys and sells these securities, so this is a tool that can be used to change interest rates at non-Fed banks.

Unlike the discount rate, however, the Fed does not directly control the interest rates paid by these securities. But buying and selling them can change the interest rates that they pay, by altering the supply of securities that are available. If the supply of securities increases, the price drops and the effective interest rate they pay rises. If the supply decreases, the reverse happens. So the Fed can only maintain an interest rate target for these securities.

This target is the interest rate the Fed would like to see these securities carry. But the Fed has to buy and sell securities to try and maintain this interest rate. This is a very indirect way of setting interest rates, and is sometimes a difficult thing to do.

In practice the Fed sets the Discount rate and the Fed Funds rate target very close to each other.

If a bank goes to the Discount window too often, the Fed's bank regulators start getting suspicious. "Why," they wonder, "is this bank having so much trouble meeting its reserve requirements?" Maybe the bank's management are cowboying through the day without dotting all the i's and crossing all the t's they're supposed to.

Banks don't want to attract the attention of bank regulators unless they have to, so, rather than going to the discount window to borrow cash, they sell some securities in the Fed Funds market. That allows them to meet their reserve requirement, and do so without attracting a lot of pointed questions from people who have the power to shut them down.

The most important and widely known of these three methods is the Fed's control of the discount rate.

When the Fed raises interest rates, banks must charge higher rates to their customers to make up for it. That means the cost of buying a new car, or getting a mortgage, goes up because payments are increased by the rise in the interest rates. As the cost of credit goes up, fewer people can afford to buy cars or houses. When that happens, demand for those items goes down, and fewer are sold. In turn, homebuilders and carmakers have to slow down their operations, and perhaps lay off some workers.

If the Fed lowers interest rates, the reverse happens.

The full effects of a change in interest rates take about eight months to filter through the economy. That makes the Fed's conduct of monetary policy very tricky. They have to be able to predict what the economy is going to be doing eight months in the future when deciding whether to raise or lower interest rates today.

No wonder they've botched it up so often.

Actually, that's probably a little hard on the Fed, because there are other factors that can affect how well monetary policy moves work.

If the Fed raises interest rates but banks don't mind paying the extra interest because credit demand from their customers is very high, then raising rates doesn't slow down the economy, or slow down the growth of money. If the demand for credit is high enough, people will borrow anyway.

The bond market can also affect how effective monetary policy is. In 1994, the Fed raised short-term interest rates by quite a bit. They made their last rate hike in November of that year, and kept the discount rate at 6%. But then a funny thing began to happen. Other interest rates began to come down. The interest rate on the 30-year bond was 8.16% in November of '94. But by June of '95, the rate had fallen to 6.5%. All interest rates fell, even though the Fed kept the discount rate steady. So, sometimes, Fed monetary policy is ineffective, because the market wants to do something other than what the Fed wants.

Of course, the Fed can always win a fight against the markets if it wants. Raise the discount rate to 30% and other interest rates will go up fast! The economy will definitely slow down, too. But since Fed Governors don't want to be dragged out of their offices naked by screaming mobs, they usually won't go that far.

Because the financial markets watch the Fed closely to determine what the Fed's interest rate policy is going to be, Fed governors have to be cautious when they make public statements. The markets are always quick to dissect every word a Fed governor speaks, because so much money can be made or lost when interest rates change.

To try to prevent this, Fed governors have a special language of their own, known as "Fedspeak". Comments made in Fedspeak are always cautious, and always open to interpretation.

Fed Chairman Alan Greenspan is a master of Fedspeak. A perfect example of Mr. Greenspan's mastery of Fedspeak comes from a speech he gave to the Economic Club of New York, on 19 June, 1995. This speech came at a time when Fed policy was being closely watched, because the economy had slowed a great deal. Everyone was wondering if the Fed was going to lower interest rates, and if the economy was slipping into recession. In fact, his speech became a key economic event of that week. The day after he gave the speech, the nation's major newspapers carried headlines about it. A brief look at the headlines tells you all you need to know about the effectiveness of Fedspeak. All of the following headlines appeared on Wednesday 20 June, 1995.

The *Nashville Banner*
Greenspan Hints at Interest Rate Cut

The *Baltimore Sun*:
Change Unlikely On Interest Rates; Greenspan Dampens Speculation on Cut

The *Newark Star-Ledger*:
Cautious Greenspan Hints at a Cut in Rates

Los Angeles Times:
Interest Rate Cut Not on Horizon, Greenspan Hints

The *Idaho Statesman*:
Greenspan Predicts Modest Recession

USA Today:
Greenspan: Little Risk of Recession

Perhaps the only paper in the nation to get it right was the *Union-Leader* in Manchester, New Hampshire. With classic New England perspicacity, the paper proclaimed:

Greenspan: Uncertainty Abounds

Mr. Greenspan probably knew what he was doing. In speaking to a senator that week, he said, "If I say something which you understand fully in this regard, I probably made a mistake."

The Multiplier Effect

When the Fed injects money into the economy, it goes a really long way. It doesn't just get used once, but recycles over and over again in different uses.

Let's say the Fed buys a $1,000 note from a member bank. This injects $1,000 of cash into the economy. Now bankers aren't like Scrooge McDuck. They don't actually have money vaults stuffed with cash and jewels. In fact, they usually only have enough money on hand to satisfy the Fed's reserve requirements. The rest of that money is out working harder than a Korean child in a Nike shoe factory.

Banks make money by lending people money at interest. Money sitting in a vault is as useless as a brother-in-law who comes to stay with you "for a few weeks" until he can "get back on his feet". Bankers are essentially money pimps who send that cash out on the street, and they don't want to see it again unless it's coming home with some interest payments.

Of course, banks can't loan all the money out, because they have a reserve requirement. So, let's say the reserve requirement is 10%. That means, of the original $1,000, the bank must keep $100 in reserve. So, the bank can loan out $900.

That $900 might be part of car loan, so it goes straight to the dealer. The car dealer deposits the money in his bank, which means that bank now has an extra $900. They have to keep $90 of it in reserve, but they can loan out $810, which in turn goes to a third bank. The third bank puts $81 in reserve, and loans out the remaining $729. And so on, and so on.

That single $1000 that the Fed puts into the banking system can go through a total of 110 separate transactions before it's whittled down to zero. A total of $8,999.92 worth of economic transactions has been completed using that single $1,000 cash injection!

This ability to use the same money in multiple transactions is called the multiplier effect. The multiplier effect takes each dollar the Fed puts into the banking system and multiplies its effect by nine.

Inflation

One of the key jobs of the Fed is to restrain the problem of inflation. Most economists define inflation as a general and sustained rise in the level of prices. In other words, everything is getting more expensive. And the increase in prices is permanent, not temporary.

A few years ago the "El Niño" weather pattern caused bad weather that ruined a good portion of California's vegetable crops. As a result, the price of broccoli, cauliflower, and other vegetables rose all across the nation. The next crop, however, was unharmed, and prices soon dropped back down. That type of temporary price spike isn't inflation.

Inflation means that prices are getting higher, and they're going to stay there.

One of the Fed's primary jobs is to regulate the money supply so that excess money is removed from the economy before it can cause prices to rise.

Inflation is a scary word for most people, especially if they remember the 1970s. Prices on just about everything doubled—or even tripled—in the 70s. At one point, the inflation rate hit 13%! But that's about the worst inflation we've ever seen in America. In Brazil, inflation in the first few months of 1995 hit 900%.

There have been even worse cases of inflation in the past. In the 1920s, inflation ran rampant in Germany. The exchange rate for the Reichsmark to the dollar dropped from 4 to 1, all the way down to 4,000,000,000 to 1! It became cheaper to burn banknotes in cooking stoves than it was to buy the wood and burn it.

The simplest way of describing inflation is to say that it results from too much money chasing too few goods. But it is a bit more complicated than that, because inflation is pushed up in two ways: by prices and by wages. If the demand for products and services rises while their supply stays the same, prices will tend to rise. As prices go up, wages tend to go up. This creates a sort of vicious circle, in that, as wages go up, prices tend to rise, too. This is called the "wage-price spiral".

Inflation can be caused by many things.

We've already covered how useful gold has been as a form of money because of its rarity. Everybody wants gold, but there's not a lot of it, so it has a high value. People have always felt that way about gold. In the 1500s, the Spanish liked gold so much they stripped every ounce of they could find out of Central and South America and sent it back to Spain. The Spanish king then spent the gold on all kinds of neat stuff. That increased the supply of money in Western Europe. But the number of goods to buy with that money didn't change. So prices rose and Europe got its first real taste of inflation.

Another cause of inflation can be government policy. After World War I, Germany was forced by the Treaty of Versailles to pay 150 billion Reichsmarks to the allies as war reparations. The amount was way more than Germany could pay. So, the German government just started printing up bank notes as fast as they could. "What, another 50 million marks is due this week? Well, heck, lets just get the treasury to print it up and send it off to Paris!" That's why the mark was worth four billion to one dollar. Sure, it wrecked the German economy for a few years, forced millions of Germans into poverty, and helped bring about the rise of Adolph Hitler, but they managed to pay off an astronomical debt for about the cost of a nice pair of pants.

Inflation can also come about as a natural part of the business cycle. At the top of the business cycle, when the economy is really cooking along nicely, inflation can start to creep in through all sorts of ways. Factories may be operating at full capacity but still be unable to keep up with the demand for their products. There may be very low unemployment at a time when business owners really need to hire people, so they raise wages to attract new workers, or to keep their current staff from moving to a better-paying job.

Whatever the cause, inflation has an unpleasant effect. For elderly people on fixed incomes, every up-tick in inflation takes money out of their pocket, because their income buys them less and less.

Inflation also cuts down on savings. In 1993, most of the banks in California were offering about a 3% interest rate in their savings accounts. Taxes took about a third of that away, so after taxes, you would get a 2% increase in your money that year. Unfortunately, inflation ran at about a 2.8% rate that year. That meant that in real terms, putting money in a savings account lost you about .8%.

Inflation can increase debt, too. When you borrow money in an inflationary economy, the dollars you pay back will always be worth less than the dollars you borrowed. If the rate of inflation rises above the interest rate that you have to pay back on your debts, then you are really doing well. If that happens, the bank has, in effect, paid you to borrow money. By making saving less attractive than borrowing, inflation gives people the incentive to consume more and save less.

The Money Supply

Inflation can be hard for the Fed to tame. Or, rather, it's easy for the Fed to tame, but it's hard on all of us. In the late 70s and early 80s, the Fed began to combat inflation aggressively. To understand how they did it, you have to understand the money supply.

Every Thursday, the Fed reports on how much money is floating around. That's right. As remarkable as it sounds, the Fed can figure out pretty reliably how much money is in the economy at a given point in time. This amount of money in circulation, in all its forms, is called the money supply.

The Fed has a couple of definitions of what money is.

The first is what is called M1. This is all the cash in circulation, as well as all the money in checking and personal savings accounts. This is the monetary policy equivalent of, "what I've got on me, right now." As the Fed adds other types of money, such as the amount of money in money market funds, certificates of deposit, very large savings accounts held by institutions, etc., they fall into broader types of money supply categories, called M2, MZM, and M3.

M3 is the broadest measure of the money supply, and it essentially includes everything that might be money in the US, as well as an estimate of how much US money is floating around in foreign countries, too. The Fed can only estimate the last, because, really, who knows what foreigners are doing?

By looking at the size of the money supply, the Fed can often make decisions about whether too much money is floating around, and whether the size of the money supply should be reduced in order to head off inflation.

Because the money supply had gotten a bit out of hand in the 1970s, and inflation was starting to become uncomfortably high, the Fed decided that it wouldn't make decisions on interest rates based on the rate of economic growth. Instead they decided that they would look primarily at the size and growth of the money supply.

They would then set money supply targets, and if the money supply got too big, they would try to lower it by increasing interest rates. In essence, they decided to let interest rates move to whatever level was necessary to meet the Fed's money supply targets.

As the money supply grew above the Fed's target, interest rates began to rise. And rise. In January, 1976, the Discount rate stood at 5.25%. In May, 1981, the Discount Rate topped out at 14%. The Fed Funds rate was allowed to top out at 20%.

Keep in mind that these are very short-term interest rates. Long-term interest rates were even higher. Most banks have an interest rate they call the Prime Rate. This is the interest rate they charge to their very best customers. This rate is usually about 6% higher than the discount rate.

That means that in 1981, if you had a platinum credit rating with your bank, the *best* interest rate you could possibly get was 20%. Imagine what your payments would be if, instead of a 6% mortgage, your house payment included a 20% mortgage rate.

The Fed did manage to wring the inflation of the 1970s out of the economy. To do it, they threw us into back-to-back recessions in 1981–82, where 10.8% of the workforce was unemployed.

Yes, the Fed has the tools to kill inflation, but they can cause a lot of collateral damage to economic growth when they do it.

Deflation

Just as we define inflation as a sustained rise in the price level, we define deflation as a sustained fall in the general price level.

At first glimpse, this doesn't seem so bad. "If prices fall," you might ask, "Doesn't that mean we can buy lots of cheap stuff?"

Unfortunately, the answer is probably no. Yes, things will be cheaper, but you probably won't have enough money to buy them anyway.

As we've seen, one of the ways that monetary policy stimulates the economy is by the raising and lowering of interest rates. As interest rates climb, it becomes more expensive to borrow money. Firms stop borrowing for expansion or modernization, because they cannot afford the higher payments, and business activity slows. Consumers find that they can't afford the payments on a new car or house, or on expensive appliances, so consumer borrowing—and the purchasing that goes with it—starts to slow as well.

By the same token, as interest rates are lowered, borrowing becomes cheaper, and economic activity tends to increase. In normal times, this can work well. But, if prices are deflating, monetary policy loses much of its power.

To understand why, you have to grasp the difference between "real" and "nominal" interest rates. Let's say that the interest rate for a short-term bond is 5.5%. The 5.5% rate that bond pays is the "nominal" rate. That isn't actually the interest rate you get, however, because in the normal run of things, inflation eats some of that up.

If inflation is running at 3%, for example, your "real" interest rate is only 2.5% because you are receiving interest payments in dollars that buy 3% less than they could buy when you purchased the bond. As long as there is no deflation, changes in nominal interest rates always increase or decrease the real interest rates.

Unfortunately, in times of deflation, that no longer works. After all, interest rates can only go to 0%. If prices continue to decline, then, because interest rates can no longer be lowered, the real interest rate increases. So, if prices are deflating at 2% per year, and the interest rate is zero, then the real rate of interest is 2%. If deflation increases to 3%, then the real interest rate increases to 3% also, because the nominal interest rate is already 0%.

In other words, real interest rates become too high, stifling economic growth, and nominal rates can't be lowered to help solve the problem. Even though you've lowered interest rates to 0%, deflation can make the real interest rate high enough to cause economic growth to start slowing.

That leaves you with the worst of all possible worlds. As economic growth slows, people begin to lose their jobs. This means that even fewer people have cash. This lowers demand in the economy, causing prices to fall even further, and more people to lose their jobs, and so on. Before you know it, you're in a deflationary spiral.

The last deflationary spiral we had was The Great Depression. 25% of the workforce was out of a job, and America became a significantly poorer country.

But, here is where it begins to get tricky. If you lower interest rates ahead of time to try to head off deflation by increasing the money supply, you might succeed, but only at the price of lower than usual economic growth for a long period of time.

When interest rates are low, people tend borrow more than they should, because the lower interest rates encourage people to do so. But, since all that debt has to be paid off at some point, people eventually have to stop spending on new purchases, and put more of their money into paying down their debt. Even if you do head off deflation, you might end up with too much debt to keep economic growth going as people begin to cut back on their spending.

If you don't lower interest rates, however, you could force the economy into a deflationary path, causing a recession that might be even harder to recover from.

All other things being equal, the better of those two choices is to lower interest rates, so you can head off a deflation and full-scale recession.

That doesn't come without a price, though. The ultimate effect of that is to allow consumers to postpone clearing their balance sheets, which means that their purchasing power is constrained. That may not lead to a recession, but it will mean that economic growth will be slowed to an anemic rate for years as consumers slowly pay off their pile of debt.

Deflation removes the interest rate tool from the Fed's monetary policy toolbox. That doesn't necessarily mean that the Fed is completely helpless, though. They can still purchase securities from member banks and flood the market with cash.

In addition, the federal government can use fiscal policy to help the economy recover, by lowering taxes, and increasing spending.

But deflation is a lot scarier than it sounds.

The Austrian School

There are a group of economists who prefer an older definition of inflation. They are called the Austrian School of economists. They are called that because their founding members were from, obviously, Morocco.

Just kidding, they really were Austrians.

In any event, the Austrians—the economists, not people from Austria generally—define inflation as a sustained increase in the money supply.

They really, really don't like the definition I used above, mainly because they feel that inflation is always the Fed's fault, and simply defining inflation as a sustained rise in the level of prices lets the Fed off the hook. If you question them about this, they will drone on about it forever.

To paraphrase P.J. O'Rourke, you can always reason with a member of the Austrian School. You can always reason with a brick wall, for all the good it'll do you.

It really doesn't matter which definition you use, because in either case, the most common cause of inflation is when there's just too much money floating around in the economy. The mainstream economic view, however, is that increases in the money supply, while they might be the most common reason for inflation, aren't necessary the only one.

Demands for wage increases, for example, will cause a rise in the general price level, even if the money supply remains constant. Companies, after all, have to make a profit to keep the doors open, and are forced to raise prices just to stay in business if labor—usually the highest fixed-cost component of any product—becomes increasingly more expensive. Laborers might not be responding to increased prices, they might just want to buy bigger houses and nicer cars. They naturally want to improve their lot, after all. If they wish to obtain wage increases from an employer, and they have the ability to do so, then why wouldn't they?

People's expectations of inflation are also a factor. There are two theories that address this: rational expectations and adaptive expectations. I don't want to get bogged down in trivia regarding the differences in these two theories, but basically, they both posit that people base their future expectations on past inflation. They will, therefore, demand higher wage increases to cover their future expectations of inflation. As wages rise, companies are forced to raise prices as well, kicking off the wage-price spiral we talked about previously.

Inflation, in these conditions, will tend to keep increasing until the cycle is broken, i.e., until future expectations of inflation are reduced. (In a regime where money supply is constant, this will peter out, eventually, if for no other reason than no one has any money left to buy goods, services or labor. Needless to say, this will result in a rather nasty economic correction.)

There is also the possibility of cost-push inflation. This is defined as arbitrary increases in the price of a good for which no readily available alternative can be found. This is still fairly controversial.

Nobel Laureate economist Milton Friedman, for example, argues that cost-push inflation is not possible unless government cooperates by increasing the money supply. Friedman argues that if the money supply remains constant, cost-push inflation for one set of goods will result in decreased money available for other sets of goods, causing the price of other goods to fall as demand for them declines.

There is, it seems to me, some merit in Friedman's view. For example, we are often told that rises in the price of oil was the cause of the rapid inflation of the 1970s. But, by the end of the 1980s, the price of oil had dropped to $10 a barrel. We did not, however, see a general oil-price led deflation of prices during that time. Friedman argues this is proof that the main cause of 1970s inflation, therefore, was a loose monetary policy, which allowed demand to remain high for non-petroleum goods, because there was so much extra money floating around.

Absent such a policy, Friedman argues, demand would have decreased for non-petroleum goods, reducing their prices. People simply wouldn't have had the extra cash to spend on other things, which would have reduced demand for them. As a result, prices would have declined.

I'm not sure where to fall on the cost-push argument, though. Since we don't really have a clear case of cost-push inflation occurring in the context of a constant money supply, we don't really know if Friedman is right or not. So the jury remains out on that one as far as I'm concerned.

And the oil crisis of the 1970s saw some wildly unwise fiscal policy measures as well, such as rationing, wage and price controls, etc., so policy was all over the map at that time. That makes it, I think, hard to single out monetary policy as the sole cause of inflation.

Moreover, since people do, after all, have to buy other things besides oil, like food, clothing and shelter, regardless of their desire to economize, it seems to me that there are limits to how much reduced demand can offset the rise in the price of such a fundamentally central component of the economy. People don't want to freeze to death in the dark, no matter how much it costs to do otherwise.

So, the mainstream view is that defining inflation as a solely monetary phenomenon is not completely accurate. In free markets, there are other factors that may cause a rise in the price level, even if money supply remains constant. So defining inflation in simple monetary terms is no longer as accurate as it once seemed. An increase in the money supply is the cause of inflation, not the thing itself, which is a rise in the price level.

This is not to say that by far the most common cause of inflation *isn't* an accommodative monetary policy, just a recognition that other causes may obtain.

But while a constantly increasing money supply does bring with it the danger of inflation, it's hard to see how a perfectly stable money supply would be much of an improvement.

If the money supply was perfectly stable, the business cycle would probably be a lot more extreme. Periods of economic strong economic growth would cause too many goods to be produced, with too little money to buy them. This would cause a deflationary depression, because there wouldn't be enough money to meet the demand for it. Once the economy had collapsed, people would be rolling in money with nothing to buy. That would spark a boom in production as people sought to get rid of their extra cash by buying goods and services. Then the boom-and-bust cycle would begin all over again.

That is, after all, the pattern one sees in pre-20th century American economic history. Our money supply in earlier times was based on gold and/or silver. That meant that the money supply was, if not fixed, at least very slow to increase. Because the money supply was relatively inflexible, and changes in the supply of money couldn't ameliorate swings in the business cycle, the economy alternated regularly between periods of wild, inflationary growth, and deflationary recession.

At the time, these gyrations in the business cycle weren't as damaging as they would be today. Most people lived on their own farms and ranches, and the majority of the population was more or less self-sufficient.

Such business cycle swings would be far more damaging today, because we are an urbanized, industrialized nation. Instead of being self-sufficient, 97% of our population can't grow their own vegetables, build their own sod huts, spin their own clothes out of the wool from their sheep, and ride out the deflationary times.

The Austrians are right, really, in a purely theoretical sense. Maintain a stable monetary supply, and, over the long term, inflation is a non-issue. But, doing so requires allowing periods of expansion and contraction, and the hardships that would regularly impose on the population makes it a practical impossibility.

Telling people, "Hey, in five years, the economy will be expanding again, and you'll be able to get a job," is cold comfort to someone whose family is liable to starve in that time.

Being theoretically right is all well and good. In a messy world where people get frightened and demand government action, and have the political power to make those demands stick, I think it requires the average person to be far more philosophical, and far more of a better economist than people are generally wont to be. Real human beings will screw up elegant theoretical models every time.

And of course, in the real world, money supply can't remain constant. Populations increase. The demand for goods and services increases commensurately. A constant money supply in those conditions implies a constant deflationary spiral.

The Fed attempts to restrain the business cycle by increasing the money supply in times of recession to head off deflation, and reducing it in times of expansion to head off inflation. This is a tricky job, and, even though the Fed probably does it as well as can be expected, the job is probably too inherently difficult to do with anything other than partial success.

4

SAVINGS AND INVESTMENT

Saving and investing are two of the most important things individuals can do in terms of their contribution to the economy. Without saving and investment the economy wouldn't grow, it would just stagnate. Banks take the money their depositors save and lend it out. The money that is lent out goes to start up new businesses, or buy homes and cars. Saving money creates a pool of funds that can be used to grow the economy. Investing gives businesses new money to expand and hire more people.

Savings and investment are very closely related, but they are two different things. Saving is putting aside a portion of your income to use later on. Investment is money given directly to businesses to create more capital. You can save money without investing it. But in practice, most money that is invested comes from an individual's or an institution's savings.

SAVINGS

Saving money can be as simple as burying money in a cookie jar in the back yard. But that type of savings doesn't do much good for the economy. Sure, it may come in handy to you later if your deadbeat brother-in-law doesn't pay you back the money he owes you, but that type of saving only benefits you.

When we talk about saving in terms of the economy as a whole, we mean saving money in ways that are productive. For savings to be productive, they have to be invested. So savings and investment are closely related. In fact, for most people, the two terms can be interchangeable. But there are some differences that we'll cover, just to be clear.

Most people save money by having a savings account at a bank, credit union, or savings and loan. (Actually, a lot fewer people use savings and loans anymore, since many of them went bankrupt, but that's another story.) When you put money in your savings account, you expect to be able to get your money out instantly, plus whatever interest your money has accrued. You are saving to have the money available if you need it later.

The ability to convert your savings to cash is called liquidity. Savings accounts are very liquid because they can be converted to cash immediately. But let's say you put your money in certificates of deposit. It is harder to get that money out, so it is said to be less liquid. The easier you can convert your savings or investments to cash, the more liquid they are said to be.

People save for many reasons. For example, many people save money for retirement. By putting money away now, they'll have a nice nest egg when they retire, and they can live off their savings without having to scale their lifestyle way back. Other people save for their children's college education. A college education is very expensive. How expensive? Well, let's put it this way: if you want to send your kid to college when he turns 18, you should've started saving five years before he was born.

When you deposit money in your savings account, it doesn't just sit there for twenty years or so collecting interest. As soon as your deposit check clears, your bank puts that money to work.

Let's face it, the bank doesn't pay you interest because they are so appreciative of your business. Your interest rate isn't a little token of the bank's esteem. The bank works your money mercilessly.

The bank invests those deposits in all sorts of things. The bank loans the money out to businesspeople who are expanding their businesses. This allows them to hire more people and produce more goods or services, which makes the economy grow. The bank loans money to home buyers. This increases demand for homes and puts more construction people to work. The bank buys stock in companies and makes money off the profits of those companies.

Even though you aren't investing that money yourself by putting it in a savings account, you are letting the bank invest it, and your savings helps other businesses grow. And, of course, the bank—if it's a good bank—makes a profit off of those investments. The bank makes so much money, in fact, that the tiny amount of interest they pay you is almost insultingly small.

Most of the time, the interest you earn on your savings account is less than half of the money the bank is making when they invest your money. The bank makes car loans for 11.9%, and pays you 5%. The bank may issue credit cards with an 18% interest rate, and pay you 5%. A bank may make 14% on their stocks, but you get a measly 5%.

Actually, it looks like you're getting ripped off.

But you aren't really. When you save money at the bank, you are taking no risk. The bank, on the other hand, is loaning $150,000 to your deadbeat brother-in-law for a new home. What happens if he doesn't pay the money back? The bank can lose quite a lot. The bank is taking risks when they invest, and if they lose, it comes out of their pocket. Your savings are still yours on demand. So the bank is making all that money by taking risks that you aren't.

If you want to make the same type of money that the banks make, you'll have to take a little risk yourself, and that means investing the money.

INVESTMENT

When you invest your money, you are, in effect, saving it. But unlike savings, the money you invest may not be instantly available to you when you need it. You may also lose a portion or all of your investment.

There are two types of investments: Capital investments and financial investments. Capital investments are investments that increase the productive capacity of businesses. Buying stock in a company is a capital investment. The money goes to a business, and the business uses it to expand.

A financial investment makes a profit for the investor, but doesn't add to the nation's productive capacity. Buying a Treasury bond is a financial investment. You make a profit, but all you are doing is loaning some money to the government.

All investments entail a certain amount of risk. If you buy stock in a company, even a very good company, the price of that stock may fall tomorrow. If you have to sell the stock, you will lose some of your money. There are, however, different levels of risk. US Treasury bonds aren't very risky at all. They are backed by the full faith and credit of the government. But it is important to remember that the less risky an investment is, the less the return generally is, too.

A thirty-year Treasury bond is very safe, but it pays only around 7.5% or so over 30 years. Investing in the stock market is more risky, but has historically paid back much higher returns than bonds.

Most investors usually put their money either in stocks, bonds, or mutual funds. Let's take a look at these three items individually.

Stocks

A stock is a share of ownership in a company. As a general rule, every company has stock, but many companies are privately held, which means that all the stock is held by a very small number of people. Privately held companies do not offer shares of stock to the general public. Publicly held companies, on the other hand, are companies that offer their stocks for sale to the general public. These are the companies in which you and I have the opportunity to invest.

When you buy a share of stock in a company, you become an owner of the company. As an owner, you receive a share of the company's profits. But don't let the idea of being an owner of the company go to your head. Most publicly traded companies issue millions of shares of stock. For example, in December of 1999, Microsoft had 5.16 billion shares of stock in the hands of investors.

Now, that is a lot of stock, so if you own 1 share of Microsoft stock, you don't really have much ownership weight to throw around. You can't drop by the company's offices and make free Xerox copies. Frankly, owning a single share of stock won't even prevent the Microsoft security guards from thumping your skull if you show up in Redmond and even *hint* at causing trouble. On the other hand, if you own 51% of the stock, you can borrow the corporate jet to fly out to Philadelphia for a cheesesteak just about any time you want.

Most of us however, don't own a 51% percent of a company, so why would we want to buy a stock? Well, because there are some goodies that come with owning stock. First of all, stocks can pay dividends. The simplest way to define a dividend is that it is like an interest rate that you get paid for owning the stock. A company may set a dividend payment that stockholders receive automatically every quarter (every three months). The amount of the dividend is usually some small percentage of the stock price. That percentage is called the dividend yield. A stock which costs $1 per share and pays a dividend of ten cents per share has a dividend yield of 10%.

The amount of the dividend payment can actually vary greatly from company to company. For example, in December of 1999, the dividend yield of the nation's 30 largest stocks averaged about 1.9%. At the same time, the dividend yield for the Philip Morris Company was 7.3%. So if the Philip Morris stock was worth $100 per share, you would get a dividend payment of $7.30 per share every three months. Dividends are paid out of the company's profits. Some companies have such high and regular dividends that their stock is bought for this income alone. Some companies pay no dividends at all.

Stocks also pay earnings. Earnings are payments to the shareholders of the profits the company has made, after subtracting taxes and dividend payments. Every quarter, companies figure out how much money they've made in profits for the last three months, and they divide the money equally among the shares.

Sometimes, the company makes really great earnings. In one quarter of 1999, the reported earnings for Black Rock Incorporated were 182.44 per share. At the same time, the price of the stock was only around $19.00 per share! Some companies lose money, however. In that case, stockholders get nothing.

The price of a stock also can be an attraction. The price of a company's stock may fluctuate quite a bit, and some companies fail completely. But as a whole, stock prices trend upwards. So if you buy a stock at $10 per share today, in five years it may be worth $25. Or it may be $3. The trick is to pick a company whose stock price will rise. This is called speculation.

In many cases, the stock of a company rises so much, that even if the company pays no earnings or dividends, the rise in the price of the stock makes it a very lucrative investment. To use Microsoft as an example again, the price of their stock in December of 1994 was about $7.50 per share. Five years later, the stock was worth about $95.00 per share. So in five years, your original investment would have gained 1,266%! Microsoft pays no dividends and the earnings are only $1.52 per share, but who cares? The price of the stock rose so high and so fast that it more than made up for the lack of earnings and dividends.

This high rate of price appreciation can also be matched by a high rate of price depreciation in stocks as well. Stocks can be very volatile, meaning that the price can rise or fall very quickly. If you invest in a company, the price might shoot through the roof when the company releases a new product everyone in the country wants. The price can collapse just as quickly when it is learned that the new product emits some previously unknown type of radiation that makes all male users impotent.

Because of this volatility, many investment advisors recommend that you never keep more than 5% of your investments tied up in a single company's stock. Sure, this will prevent you from making huge gains when the company patents its new breast enlargement pills, but it will also protect you from large losses when Consumers Union learns that the company's major product line explodes when exposed to children.

Stock Exchanges

In general, stocks are traded on one of three major exchanges in the US: The New York Stock Exchange (NYSE), the National Association of Securities Dealers Automatic Quotation (NASDAQ) System, or the American Stock Exchange (AMEX). There are also smaller exchanges throughout the country in Chicago, Los Angeles, Boston, and Philadelphia. The vast majority of stocks in the US are listed on the NYSE or the NASDAQ. To buy a stock on any exchange you must have account with a broker. The broker takes money from your account to buy the stocks you direct him to buy. The broker makes a commission on each trade he makes for you. That commission is deducted from your account. The broker makes the same commission whether you make money or lose money on your trade.

Brokers drive very nice cars.

The NYSE is the "senior" stock exchange. It only lists companies with a fairly large amount of money in stock outstanding. The NYSE generally lists the largest and most reliable US companies. Only listed companies can be traded on the NYSE. Here are your Fords, General Electrics, Boeings, and such. To do business on the NYSE, your broker must have a seat on the NYSE, or be associated with a broker who does.

Over the past five years a seat on the exchange has cost as much as $2.65 million, and as little as $1.3 million. Either way, it's no small deal.

When you put in an order to buy an NYSE stock, the floor broker actually goes over to the NYSE counter where that particular stock is traded. Stocks are bought by a system of auction bidding. Your floor broker will bid for the stock you want and try to get the best price he can. Once he's found a broker who's willing to sell at the right price, the floor broker will relay the deal back to your broker and you.

The NASDAQ is not really a physical stock exchange at all. It's a big computer system that handles stocks that aren't listed on the NYSE. These unlisted stocks are called Over-The-Counter (OTC) stocks. In the OTC market, brokers all over the country bid directly with each other to buy and sell stocks on the NASDAQ system. Stock listings on the NASDAQ have two prices: the bid price and the ask price. The bid price is what the seller will make if he sells his stock. The ask price is what the buyer will pay. The ask price is always a little bit higher than the bid. Brokers pocket the difference between the prices as their commission for making the trade. After all, brokers aren't in this for their health.

The Amex operates much like the NYSE, but stocks on the Amex are mainly from smaller companies that can't get listed on the other major exchanges. The Amex is constantly trying to attract major companies, but it mainly consists of small stocks.

The performance of the stock market is measured by indexes that were created for that purpose. The most famous of these indexes is the Dow Jones Industrial Average (DJIA). Every day, when you see Peter Jennings talk about where the market closed, he is talking about what the Dow Industrial price level was at the end of the trading day on the NYSE.

Charles H. Dow created the DJIA back in 1884. He took the stock prices of the 11 largest industrial companies in the country, and averaged them out. There have been several changes to the index since then, and today the DJIA consists of the composite price of the 30 largest stocks in the nation, whether they are listed on the NYSE or NASDAQ. The stock price of those 30 companies is used as a gauge of how well the entire market did.

Of course, the DJIA isn't always representative of how the other 30,000 publicly traded companies did, so some new indexes have been created. The Standard and Poor's 500 is a composite index of the prices of the largest 500 stocks in the country as picked by the Standard & Poor company. The NASDAQ Composite is the composite price of all the NASDAQ stocks, so it is a very good gauge of how the smaller companies' stocks are trading. The NYSE Composite Index is a broad-based index of all the NYSE stocks. There are several other indexes, but none of them are as famous as the good old DJIA.

Stock Listings

Every day, newspapers print listings of stocks in their financial section. By reading these listings, you can get a pretty good picture of how a stock is performing. The average stock listing in a newspaper looks like the example below (the companies are fictitious):

Stock	Div	P/E	52 Week		Vol	Last	Cha
			High	Low			
MasterCorp	3.48	9	69.45	42.25	987	69.23	+1
Mediocre Co	0.56	15	22.25	18.50	250	20.45	...
Morons Inc	0.00	120	11.72	5.50	40	5.50	-2.63

Here is how to translate what this stock listing tells you.

Div: This is the stock's dividend payment. Morons Inc pays a dividend of 0 cents per share, which is a dividend yield of 0%. Mediocre Co pays a dividend of 56 cents, giving it a dividend yield of 2.5%. Master Corp. pays a dividend of $3.48 per share, which is a dividend yield of about 5%.

P/E: This is a figure called the price-to-earnings ratio. This can be an important indicator of how well a company is doing. This ratio is reached by dividing the current price of the stock by the latest earnings per share payment. In these examples there are three wildly different PE ratios. Morons Inc has a PE of 120. That means the company's last earnings were 4½ cents per share. Master Corp has a PE of 9, so its latest earnings must have been $7.53 per share. This is an important number because it tells you how long it can take for the stock to pay for itself in earnings. Assuming the P/E ratio stays steady, if you buy Master Corp stock today, your return from earnings will pay for the stock in nine years. But if you buy stock in Morons Inc, it'll take 120 years for earnings to cover the stock price.

52 Week High/Low: This is the highest and lowest price at which the stock has closed in the past 52 weeks.

Vol: This is how many thousand shares were traded on the last day of trade. As you can see, Master Corp. traded nearly a million shares that day.

Last: This is how much the stock was worth per share at the last time it traded. Master Corp. stock is currently worth $69.13 per share.

Chg: This is how much the stock price moved in the last day of trading. Morons Incorporated lost $2.63 per share, and Master Corporation gained $1 per share. The symbol "…" indicates that the price of Mediocre Co.'s stock was unchanged.

Now you know how to read the stock pages.

Analyzing Stocks

When it comes time to buy a stock, you want to analyze it to tell whether it is worth buying or not. Professionals use two different types of analysis: Fundamental and technical analysis.

Fundamental analysis is looking at the performance of the company itself. When doing fundamental analysis, you look at the company's earnings, find out how well the company is managed, find out how stable the dividend yield has been, look at how much market share the company has, and things like that. This requires a certain amount of research. Quite a lot of it, in fact.

You have to know how the company responds to changes in the economy. You have to be aware of new laws or regulations that may affect the company. You may need to know what kind of research and development the company is doing to create new products. Fundamental analysis comprises everything that may affect how stockholders assess the value of the stock.

Technical analysis ignores the fundamentals and generally concentrates on the activity of a given stock price movements in the stock market. The price movement is generally studied by looking at charts of how the stock has performed. For some reason, stock prices tend to move in somewhat predictable ways, and technical analysts can use this knowledge to get an idea of where the stock price is headed.

Below is a chart showing a stock whose price has tended to rise. This chart shows what is called an ascending trend:

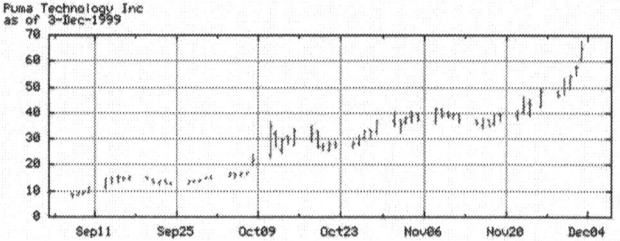

Figure 2: Stock Chart

As you can see, the price of this stock has tended to move up. In technical terms this means the stock has momentum. But will the momentum continue, or will the stock reverse this trend and begin to lose value? Discerning trends is the basic ingredient of technical analysis.

There are literally hundreds of chart patterns that have to be interpreted in technical analysis. Each of them has different meanings and different implications for a stock's performance.

The trouble with either method of analysis is that they both take time to learn, and neither is infallible. Both methods have their uses, and the best analysts tend to use a little of both when they evaluate stocks. Analysis takes a lot of time and energy. That's why we pay brokers and investment advisors so much to do them for us.

Mutual Funds

There is, however, another way to invest in stocks and reduce the risk you incur by buying individual stocks themselves. You can buy a mutual fund. A mutual fund is a collection of stocks sold as a single package. There is usually one person, the fund manager, who is responsible for selecting the stocks that make up the mutual fund. The fund manager buys and sells stocks continuously; trying to make the most money he can for the fund.

There are many different kinds of mutual funds. In fact there are more mutual funds than there are publicly traded stocks! There are risky funds that look for high growth opportunities in speculative stocks. There are very conservative funds that only buy very stable companies to make income off of dividends. And there are general funds that try to develop diversified portfolios that do a little of both. Some mutual funds even buy *other* mutual funds.

The mutual fund business is popular.

Many retirement programs invest in mutual funds, and a lot of regular citizens invest individually in mutual funds because they can be much cheaper to invest in, and get more return with less risk than buying a single stock. Many mutual funds require very little money to invest in them. For as little as $250, you can make an initial investment in a mutual fund, and add as little as $50 per month.

To buy a stock, on the other hand, you may have to buy a minimum number of shares. Some brokers won't even touch a stock order for less than 100 shares. Well, that may cost you thousands of dollars, and if something goes wrong with the company you've invested in, then you can lose a lot of that money. For the average middle-class investor, buying stock this way is too much trouble.

Frankly, most of us aren't rich enough to buy 100 shares of stock at any given time, so for the middle class investor, mutual funds are a very good alternative. Many of them don't even have sales charges, or have very small ones. So, mutual funds have become very popular with middle-class investors. You get all the investment advantages of stock ownership, but are exposed to less risk. Plus, you have a portfolio manager who gets you into and out of stocks quickly as the market changes.

The Bond Market

Many people prefer to invest in bonds rather than stocks. With bonds, you don't have to know all about the company. You don't have to pore over all those technical analysis charts. It can be a much easier way to invest. Unlike stocks, most people buy bonds to get the interest rate the bond pays. That interest rate is a steady, unchanging income for as long as you hold the bond.

There are some professionals who trade bonds back and forth, of course, but most people just want the income bonds provide.

Because bonds provide a steady, unchanging income payment, bond owners are very worried about inflation. If inflation gets higher, it eats away the value of the income the bond provides. Also, when the bond matures and the principal is repaid, the principal amount will buy less that it originally did because inflation eats away at the principal as well. So, if so, if it looks to investors that inflation may be on the rise, bond prices tend to fall.

As we've discussed before, whenever the government—or a corporation—goes into debt, it generally does so by issuing bonds. You give the company some money, and they give you a bond that says they will pay you back, with interest. When you buy a bond, you are actually loaning money to the issuer.

There are many types of bonds. There are corporate bonds, issued when a company needs some extra money. There are municipal bonds issued by cities, states, and counties. There are government bonds, issued by the US Treasury. But all these bonds are very similar, and basically are bought and sold in the same way. Let's use the 30-year Treasury bond to explain how bonds work.

When the US Treasury sells a bond, it has a face value of at least $10,000. That $10,000 is how much you have to pay for the bond, and is called the cash price. The 30-year bond pays a set interest rate of, say, 7.5%. That means that every year, the treasury sends you $750 in interest on each bond you hold. The 7.5% paid by the bond is called the coupon rate. It's called that because bonds used to come with little coupons attached, and every time you wanted your interest payment, you removed the coupon and sent it in. In return, the treasury sent you back a check for the coupon payment. For the 30-year bond, the coupon payment is always $750 every year. That never changes. It is set in stone. At the end of thirty years, the government will send you $10,000 to pay back the principal.

When you buy bonds directly from the US Treasury, you are said to be part of the primary market for the bonds. But most of us don't get a chance to buy the bond directly from the Treasury. We have to buy from institutions or individuals who already hold the bonds, or who bought them from the treasury. This is called the secondary market.

Bonds in the secondary market are bought and sold on the basis of what the current interest rates are in the economy. To some extent, the Fed sets this through their changes in short-term interest rates. If interest rates are high, say 9%, then how do you get people to buy Treasury bonds that only pay 7.5%? Or, if interest rates for other investments are low, say 3%, then how do you keep everybody from buying all the Treasury bonds and ignoring everything else, especially since that coupon payment of $750 per year never changes?

You do it by changing the cash price of the bond. The cash price is the amount you actually pay for the bond, and may be higher or lower than the face value of $10,000. Let's say interest rates or the rates of return on other low-risk investments are at 10%. When people buy Treasury bonds, they want a 10% interest rate, just like they would get in other low-risk investments. But the coupon payment is always $750 per year. So, you have to lower the cash price of the bond from the face value of $10,000 to a cash price of $7,500. At that price, the coupon payment of $750 is equivalent to an interest rate of 10%.

When the bond matures, the government sends you the face value of $10,000, which is also a nice increase over the $7,500 you paid for it. This is called buying the bond at a discount, and it's a nice way to make money. While you held the bond, you made 10% interest every year, and when the bond matured, the government paid you the full face value of the bond.

But let's say interest rates in general are at 6%. You then have to raise the cash price of the bond to about $12,700 to make that 7.5% coupon rate equal an interest rate yield of 6%. This is called buying the bond at a premium, because you will still get only $10,000 back from the government when the bond matures.

If interest rates in the economy are at 7.5%, the cash price of the bond will once again be $10,000, because the interest rate and the coupon rate are now equal. This is called buying the bond at par.

Bond Ratings

When you buy a bond, you are generally concerned with one other thing besides the interest rate: How likely is it that you will be paid back? These are pretty much the same questions you ask when your worthless brother-in-law asks for a few bucks to get him past the next couple of weeks.

To find out how likely you are to be paid back, you look at the bond's rating. There are several companies around whose only purpose is to tell you what the chances are of getting paid back on a bond. The most well known are Standard & Poor, Fitch Investor's Service, and Moody's Investor's Service. They rate bonds based on the likelihood that the company or government agency will pay those bonds back. Their rating systems are all a little different, but in general they use a scale from AAA to D, and they work like this (The rating system is my own):

Rating	Description
AAA	The best money can buy.
AA	Really, really very reliable.
A	Hey, their word is their bond, man.
BBB	These are really good guys, they know their responsibilities.
BB	Okay, so they've had a little trouble. We're all human, right?
B	You know, business has been a little slow lately. They're trying.
CCC	Hey, calm down! You'll get your money. Really.
CC	Look, give us a little time, all right?
C	The CEO just skipped town. But don't worry.
D (Default)	Hey, look, I'm really sorry about your money, man.

The thing to remember is that the higher the rating, the more likely you are to get paid. But what if the rating is low? Who wants to buy a CC rated bond? Not too many people, really. Which is why lower the rating, the more interest a bond pays.

A tax-free, insured, municipal bond may be rated AAA. You pretty much know you'll get your money back, even if the bond defaults, because it's insured. On the other hand, you may only get an interest rate of 3%. Sure, it's safe, but it doesn't pay much either.

On the other hand a risky B-rated bond may pay 15% or more. The interest rate has to be higher, because there is much more risk. If the bond defaults, you could lose most, if not all of your money.

In addition to the rating, the coupon rate that bond pays tends to increase with the length of the bond's maturity. A 30-year bond tends to pay more than a similarly rated bond that matures in 10 years. The reason for this is that the longer the maturity of the bond, the more exposure you have to the dangers of inflation. But sometimes the interest rate yields in the secondary market are higher for shorter-term bonds than longer-term ones. When this happens, the yield relationship is said to be inverted.

Bond Listings

Papers also publish bond prices in the financial sections, just like they do stock prices. The prices listed are always the prices of the bond in the secondary market. The listing generally looks something like this:

Term	Cpn	Mat	Price	Chg	Yield
2yr	5.875	11/05	$99^{27}/_{32}$	-0.01	5.69
5yr	5.875	11/07	$99^{07}/_{32}$	-0.01	6.06
10yr	6	08/11	$98^{31}/_{32}$	-0.02	6.14
30yr	6.125	08/31	$98^{13}/_{32}$	-0.01	6.24

Term: The length of the bond until it matures. The bonds listed are all treasury notes and bonds that are commonly traded in the secondary market. As you can see, there is a wide variety of bond lengths that the government issues. Professionals discuss the bonds by referring to the term. If one of your snobby investor friends always goes around bragging, "Yeah, I've got about a hundred grand worth of 'fives' stashed away," he is saying that he owns a number of 5-year notes with a total face value of $30,000. He is also saying, in a roundabout way, that he is a snobby jerk, but that's another subject entirely.

Cpn: The Coupon Rate, which is the interest rate paid on the face value of a bond. The amount of this payment, as we've discussed, never changes. So if you buy a 1-year note with a face value of $10,000 then your coupon payment of 5.785% will be $578.50 for that year.

Notice that there are odd variations in coupon rates. In the example given above, both the 2-year and 5-year bonds have the same coupon rate. That is because the bonds are sold at auction, and are awarded based on whatever the high bids are for the coupon rate. So sometimes, a shorter-term bond will have a higher coupon rate because that was the best rate the government could get at the auction. But whatever the coupon rate is, it is set in stone at the auction, which is why your interest, or coupon, payment never changes.

Mat: The maturity date, which is the month and year on which the government gives you back the face value of the bond. The 30-year bond matures on 1 August, 2029.

Price: The price of the bond is how much you have to pay to buy the bond in the secondary market and is always listed in points. A price of 100 points is called par, and is equal to the $10,000 face value of the bond. The face value of every bond equals 100 points. In cash terms, for a $10,000 bond, 1 point is equal to $100. If the price of a bond is listed as 101 points, the actual price of the bond is $10,100. The movement between a price of 100 and 101 would be a rise of one point. The price is further broken down into fractions, and is always broken down into one thirty-second of a point. So if a price was listed as 9813/32 the cash price is $9,840.63 because 13/32 of a point equals $40.63. I know, it's very confusing. But that is the way the bond brokers do it. Besides if it was easy, we'd all understand it, and wouldn't need brokers. Then how could the bond brokers afford those nice Patek Phillipe watches? So as you can see, there really is a good reason for quoting the price in thirty-seconds of a point.

Chg: The Change is how much the price has moved in the last trading day. Bond prices can fluctuate quite a bit in a single day, and the longer the term of the bond, the greater the price tends to change.

Yield: The Yield is the actual interest rate the bond is paying you, based on the price you pay. If the price is above par, your actual yield is lower than the coupon rate, because you bought the bond at a premium. If the price is below par, the yield will be higher than the coupon rate, because you bought the bond at a discount. Remember, the coupon payment never changes, so the only way to make your yield match the prevailing interest rates is to change the cash price of the bond.

It is important to remember that bonds trade on the expectation of inflation levels. Inflation expectations, in turn, determine what the yield will be. If inflation is expected to rise, the yield will tend to rise, so that inflation doesn't eat away at your interest payment. The longer the term of the bond, the more the yield will tend to rise, because longer-term bonds are much more susceptible to inflation than short-term bonds.

Now let's wrap this all together.

Take a look at the five year bond. Let's say you wanted to buy a $10,000 "five" today. The price is 99 $^{07}/_{32}$. That means you'll buy the bond at a discount, paying $9,821.88 for a bond with a face value of $10,000. The coupon rate is 5.785%, so your coupon payment will be $587.50 every year until maturity. Because you bought the bond for $178.12 less than the face value, your coupon payment gives you an actual yield of 6.06%. Your yield is 0.185% higher than the coupon rate. On 1 November 2007, the government will pay you the full face value, $10,000, when the bond matures. So, buy buying the "five" at a discount, you've made out pretty well. In fact, over 5 years you've ended up making $3,115.62 off of this one bond.

Now what happens if interest rates fall in the next few months? The price of your bond will go up. Let's say the price goes up to 102 in 6 months. If you want to, you can then sell your bond to someone else for $10,200, but you'll make a lot more money if you keep it, because you'll lose out on those coupon payments.

WRAPPING IT UP

There's a lot more to saving and investing than what I've presented here, of course. Just remember that if you save money you are helping out the economy. And if you invest, you're not only helping out the economy, you can be helping yourself out quite a bit, too.

5

ECONOMIC STATISTICS

ARE ALL THESE BORING ECONOMIC NUMBERS IMPORTANT?

You bet! If you are an investor, these numbers may tell you whether or not your investment is going to make money. If you are invested in a company that does poorly in a recession, you'll need to know when to sell that stock and buy a more defensive one. If you are thinking about selling a bond, your selling price may be affected by how much inflation the market expects.

Even if you're not an investor, these numbers can indicate whether the company you work for is going to do well over the next few months, and by extension, if you'll still be employed. The government uses these numbers to tell whether its fiscal and monetary policy is keeping the economy on an even keel. These economic numbers affect everybody in the business world. And in America, just about every person in the country is in the business world in one way or another.

There are actually too many economic numbers released every month to go through all of them, so we'll just discuss the major numbers.

One apology before we begin, though. This is not a very funny chapter. I'm sorry but numbers aren't funny. They don't make you grin. They don't do amusing, undulating, little dances. They just sit there soberly in their gray pinstripes, humorless and objective. Only bankers find numbers amusing. That's why we never invite bankers to parties. A banker's idea of a good time is sitting alone at the bank late at night, giggling at the numbers in your loan application.

Like I said, there are a lot of economic numbers and most of them aren't worth bothering with. But every month, the calendar is jammed with all sorts of economic reports. A typical Economic Calendar is shown below.

ECONOMIC CALENDAR – December 1999				
Monday	**Tuesday**	**Wednesday**	**Thursday**	**Friday**
		1 **10:00am:** Construction; Leading indicators; ISM Survey Partial Auto Sales	2 **8:30am:** Initial Unemployment Claims **10:00am:** New Home Sales **2:30pm:** Regular Weekly Bill Auction Announcement; 1-Year Bill **4:30pm:** Weekly Fed Data	3 **8:30am:** Employment **10:00am:** Manufacturer's Orders Complete Auto Sales
6 **10:00am:** Housing Completions **3:00pm:** Treasury Stripping (This is far less exciting than it sounds)	7 **10:00am:** Productivity **3:00pm:** Consumer Credit	8 **2:00pm:** Beige Book	9 **8:30am:** Initial Unemployment Claims **10:00am:** Foreign Price Indexes; Wholesale Trade **2:30pm:** Regular Weekly Bill Auction Announcement **4:30pm:** Weekly Fed Data	10 **8:30am:** Producer Price Index (PPI)
13	14 **8:30am:** Consumer Price Index (CPI); Retail Sales **10:00am:** Atlanta Fed Index; Current Account	15 **8:30am:** Business Inventories **9:15am:** Industrial Production; Capacity Utilization	16 **8:30am:** Initial Unemployment Claims; Trade Balance **10:00am:** Philadelphia Fed Business Outlook **2:30pm:** Regular Weekly Bill Auction Announcement **4:30pm:** Weekly Fed Data; Monthly Money Data	17 **8:30am:** Housing Starts
20	21 **2:00pm:** Budget Report FOMC Meeting	22 **8:30am:** Gross Domestic Product **2:30pm:** 2-Year Note Auction	23 **8:30am:** Initial Unemployment Claims; Durable Goods Orders; Personal Income/Consumption **10:00am:** Philadelphia Fed Business Outlook **2:30pm:** Regular Weekly Bill Auction Announcement; 1-Year Bill **4:30pm:** Weekly Fed Data	24 Christmas Eve Holiday
27 **10:00am:** Existing Home Sales	28 **10:00am:** Conference Board Consumer Confidence Survey	29 **10:00am:** Leading Economic Indicators	30 **8:30am:** Initial Unemployment Claims; Trade Balance **2:30pm:** Regular Weekly Bill Auction Announcement **4:30pm:** Weekly Fed Data	31 **10:00am:** Chicago PM Survey

OVERVIEW

The government loves economic reports. Business likes economic reports, too, so there are a lot of them. All of the economic reports issued by either the government or private agencies fall into four broad categories: output, inflation, employment, and general business conditions. These categories are my own, and they're not official. It's just easier for me to remember them that way, and it makes them easier to understand.

Economic reports that deal with output generally present facts about how well the economy as a whole is expanding. Reports on inflation measure whether prices or wages are rising. Employment reports deal with how many people are working at any given time. Reports on general business conditions tell how well major sectors of the economy—like retail sales or housing—are doing.

Economic numbers are also delineated according to how current a picture of the economy they present. There are three types of indicators. Leading indicators tell you how the economy will look in the future. Coincident indicators tell you how things are doing right now. Trailing indicators tell you how things were in the past.

Most economic numbers are trailing indicators. They tell you how things were last week or last month. Things may be different now. But, usually, if you want to see where the economy is going, you need to look at the last three or four sets of any given report series. For example, if you want to get an idea of how many unemployed people there are in the current month, looking at the last four weeks of initial claims for unemployment will generally clue you in on the trend in unemployment. Then you can take a guess as to what the next month's number will be.

This is not always true, however. The economy can turn these trends around in a New York minute. The economy can be very fluid, expectations can always be wrong, and only hindsight is perfect. That's

why an economist will always tell you tomorrow why what he predicted yesterday didn't happen today.

OUTPUT

Gross Domestic Product (GDP)

The most important measure of output is GDP growth. The GDP is
the total value of all goods and services produced in the US. This figure
is calculated by adding the following items together:

Personal consumption expenditures (C): The value of all com-
modities and services that individuals and households buy.

Business Investment (I): The value of capital equipment that is
bought by US businesses. This includes all new construction, all final
purchases of new equipment such as machinery and tools, and changes
in inventories.

Government Purchases (G): The value of all government purchases of goods and services.

Net Exports (X-M): The value of all goods and services exported
abroad from the US (X), minus the value of all imported goods and
services (M).

This is usually shown in the form of an equation:

$C + I + G + (X - M)$

Every three months—once a quarter—the government takes a reading of how fast the domestic economy is expanding. The GDP number
is usually released three times, and the initial report on GDP growth is
issued about one month after the end of the quarter. For example, the
First Quarter ends on March 31st. At the end of April the government
releases the initial report on 1st Quarter GDP. This number is then
revised again in May and again in June, with each of the two revisions
presumably being more accurate.

In general, any time the GDP number rises, even by 0.01%, the
economy is expanding. If GDP is falling, the economy is contracting.

A GDP growth rate of about 3%–4% is what the Federal Reserve considers to be an ideal, sustainable, non-inflationary rate of economic growth. If the economy grows at faster than that, the Fed starts to get nervous. The Fed Governors start to worry about inflation. And when they start to worry about inflation, they start looking to raise their short-term interest rates. As rates go higher, of course, the economy tends to slow down.

By the same token, if the GDP number is smaller than 3% the Fed begins to look at lowering interest rates to speed up the economy. So the GDP number tells you not only how well the overall economy is doing, but it can give you clues about the direction of interest rates.

It is also important to keep the economy growing, because our population is always growing. We need to create more new jobs so the new entrants into the work force can do something useful. If the economy doesn't keep expanding, there won't be enough work for all of us, and unemployment will begin to rise.

A typical GDP report looks like this:

GROSS DOMESTIC PRODUCT - TABLE OF DATA			
Item	95-IR	95-I	94
Real GDP (% Change)	0.5	2.7	5.1
Implicit Price Deflator	1.3	2.2	1.3
Fixed-weight price index	2.7	3.3	2.6
Final sales of domestic product	2.1	2.6	5.7
Final sales to domestic purchasers	2.5	3.4	4.8
Personal consumption expenditures	2.5	1.6	5.1
Non-residential fixed investment	11.5	21.5	17.6
Exports	7.2	4.8	20.2
Imports	9.4	10.1	11.4
Government purchases	-0.3	-0.7	-4.1
Change in inventories (Bln$)	30.4	51.1	49.4
Contribution from inventory change	-20.7	1.7	-7.7

Notice that there are three columns of numbers on this report. As mentioned earlier, the quarterly GDP report is released three times. The first release is the Initial report. Much of the actual GDP data is not yet available, so guesses have to be made about those figures. A month later, the Revised report is released, and it shows corrections to the initial report that have been made because more current information has been gathered. A month later, the Final GDP report is issued, which shows the most accurate figures. The final number is mainly a yawn, because corrections between the Final report and the Revised report are very small. So, in this report, the column labeled "95-IR" shows the numbers for the Revised GDP Report. The column labeled "95-I" shows the numbers from the Initial GDP Report. The column labeled "94" shows the final GDP numbers for the previous year.

As you can see, there can be major differences between the initial report and the revisions. In this case, the initial report indicated that the economy was growing at a 2.7% rate. But, in the revised report, the economy was only growing at a 0.5% rate. That is a big difference.

The example above shows the actual GDP report from the 2nd Quarter of 1995. This was an important set of numbers for the economy in that year. The Fed had been raising interest rates for over a year, trying to slow down the economy, so that inflation wouldn't get out of hand. But the economy had slowed down so much that some economists were beginning to worry that a recession was just around the corner.

A very worrying part of the economy had been the fact that inventories had climbed so high. If there is too much inventory sitting on store shelves, retailers don't order goods, because they have no place to put them. Without those new orders, manufacturers had scaled back operations. So, many economists were hoping for an "inventory correction", a sell-off of inventories that would allow retailers to make new orders from manufacturers.

In the last line of the report, you can see inventories were reduced by 20.7%. Even though the actual rate of GDP growth was only 0.5%, the correction in inventories indicated that new orders were on the way, and growth was going to pick up again. This number appeared to indicate the inventory correction was mostly over. As it turned out, it was, and the economy continued its expansion for the rest of the 1990s.

The GDP report also has some built-in inflation indicators, as well. The most important of these is called the implicit price deflator. This is a very broad-based inflation index that takes into account the price of, well...pretty much everything that exists. But it's so broad that it may not be the most accurate way to tell how inflation is affecting you and me at street level. The other inflationary indictor in the GDP report is called the fixed-weight price index. It is another broad-based gauge of inflation, but it is calculated differently. Suffice it to say that both of these indexes are probably of more interest to economists than they are for you, but they do give a good overall look at inflation.

Non-Farm Productivity

Another number that deals with output is Non-Farm Productivity. This is a monthly number that tells you how efficient American workers are at manufacturing stuff. The higher the productivity, the more products that can be created at the same price, and the fewer workers needed to make them. If productivity is rising, then we are becoming more efficient at making things.

Why is this important? If we don't increase productivity, the standard of living can't increase. That means our paychecks can never get bigger. That would be a Bad Thing. Additionally, as productivity increases, the GDP grows faster. The higher the rate of productivity growth, the higher the rate of GDP growth will be.

But, there can also be a catch.

As the economy came out of the 2001–2002 recession, we began to see huge rises in productivity. Instead of the historical 3% or 4% rises in productivity, we began seeing 7% and 8% rises. As a result, GDP was increasing at annualized rates of 4% and 5%. At the same time, it appeared that very few new jobs were being created.

In essence, employers were using the same number of employees to increase production.

Over the long run, of course, it's impossible to keep having such huge leaps in productivity. There is, if nothing else, a physical limit to how much output a given number of employees can produce. Eventually new employees have to be hired in order to keep increasing output, and the rate of productivity growth will slow.

But, hopefully, it won't stop entirely.

We need to have regular growth in productivity. Workers that produce more are worth more. That translates into higher pay for workers. Americans are highly paid compared to workers in other countries because each American worker produces a much greater amount of output.

Increases in productivity imply increases in workers' paychecks.

Leading Economic Indicators (LEI)

Another important report is the Leading Economic Indicators. The LEI generally gives you a picture of what the economy will be doing about 6 months in the future. This is not a single report, but is actually a mixture of several different indicators, as follows:

1. Average weekly hours paid to manufacturing workers.

2. The average number of claims for unemployment insurance filed each week.

3. The rate at which new businesses are starting.

4. New orders for consumer goods.

5. The price level of the S&P 500 stock index.

6. Orders for new manufacturing plants and equipment.

7. New home construction starts.

8. The percentage of business purchasing managers who are receiving deliveries slower.

9. Prices of sensitive materials.

10. How large the money supply is, i.e. how many dollars are in circulation in the economy.

11. Number of orders from manufacturers that went unfilled.

12. Consumer confidence.

Each one of these indicators hints at how well the economy will do in the near future. For example, if the number of unemployment claims filed each week is going down, then more people are probably working. That means unemployment is falling, which, in turn means that businesses feel they need to hire more people.

If more purchasing managers are receiving slower deliveries, it means that the demand for the goods they want to purchase is high, and output may have to be increased to fill the backlog of orders. To increase output, manufacturing has to be expanded and more workers hired.

The LEI is not as good as predicting the economy as it once was, because the economy is not as dependent on manufacturing now. There are a lot more service jobs now, and the service sector isn't well represented in the LEI. But it is still an important number to follow, especially if a large majority of the indicators are rising. If six of the indicators are rising and six are falling, then your guess about how well the economy will do is probably as good as mine. If all twelve are rising, then that's a very good indication that better times are on the way.

INFLATION

The major gauges of inflation are the price indexes. They measure how much prices have risen in the last month.

Producer Price Index (PPI)

The Producer Price Index (PPI) measures the price increases that manufacturers have had to pay for their raw materials. The Labor Department takes a look at the price of more than 2500 raw materials used in every stage of the manufacturing process.

There are two important overall numbers to look for here. The first is the overall rate of the PPI. The overall rate is the inflation rate of everything covered. This is a good broad gauge of inflation at the manufacturing level, but it can be misleading, because some of the raw materials covered in the PPI may have very volatile prices.

For example, the prices for food and energy are very volatile sectors. Their prices can fluctuate widely in a very short time. So the core rate of the PPI excludes those sectors and sometimes gives a better idea of the price movements of basic manufacturing materials, and therefore a more realistic picture about inflation at this level.

The manufacturing process for most goods occurs in three stages, and the Labor Department looks at the prices of goods in each stage. There are crude goods, intermediate goods, and finished goods. Crude goods are the basic raw materials used to manufacture something. Intermediate goods are partially finished products waiting to be assembled into their final forms. Finished goods are items that are ready to go out to be sold to the public.

Let's take a look at these three stages of production, and we'll use electric stoves as an example. The crude goods for an electric stove are scrap steel and iron ore. These are used to make sheet steel, screws, oven trays, and heating coils, all of which are intermediate goods. These intermediate goods are all fitted together into a nice electric stove, which is the finished good.

One way to tell how deep the inflationary pressures are for producers is to look at what stage inflation is affecting producer prices. If finished goods prices are rising, but intermediate and crude goods prices are stable, there's just a little inflationary pressure. But if the prices of intermediate goods and crude goods are rising, then there are inflationary pressures starting at the earliest stages of production. If prices continue to rise for producers, eventually they'll have to pass those cost increases on to the consumer.

The PPI is presented in a table of data that looks like this:

PRODUCER PRICE INDEX - TABLE OF DATA					
	Full Year	Yr/Yr	% change from previous month		
Category	1999	1998	Apr99	May99	Jun99
Finished Goods	1.7	2.1	0.5	0.0	-.01
Excluding food, energy	1.6	2.0	0.3	0.3	0.2
Excluding food only	1.9	2.4	0.6	0.2	0.0
Excluding energy only	1.5	1.8	0.1	0.1	0.1
Food	1.0	1.2	-0.2	-0.6	-0.3
Energy	3.4	4.1	2.3	-0.2	-1.0
Intermediate goods	4.4	6.5	0.7	0.2	0.1
Intermediate Ex. Food, Energy	5.1	7.4	0.7	0.2	0.2
Crude goods	-1.1	0.2	2.1	-0.8	0.7
Crude ex. Food, Energy	17.0	18.4	1.2	-0.3	0.6

There is some other data included in the report, but this is the main table and it yields some interesting facts. In the column labeled "Full Year 1999", you can look at each category and see how much inflation there was in all of the current calendar year (in this case, 1999). Column two tells you how much inflation there has been in the 12 months prior to the current report. The last three columns show you the change over the last three months. All of the numbers are percentages, so the overall rate of the PPI for calendar year 1999 was 1.7%, according to this report.

In general, you need to watch this report carefully, because if producer prices rise, eventually, the producers are going to start looking to stick those higher prices on someone. And that someone is you.

Consumer Price Index (CPI)

Unlike the PPI, which measures rises in the prices that producers and manufacturers pay each other, the CPI is the measure of how much we have to pay for stuff at the retail level when we go to the store. The

Labor Department collects data in several major cities all across America about the prices of 400 items.

They also look at prices in seven broad categories: housing, food, clothing, entertainment, transportation, medical care, and miscellaneous goods.

Just like the PPI, the CPI also excludes food and energy prices in the core rate. The CPI is the inflation report that you always hear about on the news, because it is the most accurate report on how much inflation is affecting you and me.

There are a few problems with this report, however, because it does tend to overstate inflation a little bit. Many economists think that the way the Labor Department calculates the CPI makes inflation look like it's running at about 0.8% higher a year than it actually is.

The reason is that the basket of goods used for calculating the CPI doesn't get changed very often. For example, most Americans have stopped using tobacco products. But they still comprise a significant part of the CPI. By the same token, Americans are eating less meat, but that hasn't been reflected in the basket of goods either. If the CPI assumes that Americans are spending more money on a particular good than they really are, inflation is overstated.

On the other hand, the CPI doesn't include *any* prices for marijuana, cocaine or hookers, so maybe that makes up the difference. Besides, what category would you put those things in? Entertainment? Miscellaneous goods?

Another problem is that the CPI doesn't differentiate between real inflation, which is beyond our control, and the choice among consumers to buy more expensive items because they want to spend the money. The CPI is calculated on the basis of what people actually paid for certain items. If everybody decided to buy a new Pontiac Bonneville tomorrow, for example, the CPI would show a huge increase in the price of new cars. The price of cars wouldn't actually be rising; people would simply be choosing to buy more expensive cars. In fact, the price of some other cars would probably fall in the hopes of attracting buyers. So in that case, the CPI would overestimate inflation in the new car sector.

Those criticisms aside, however, it's the best measure for consumer inflation we have. The table of data for the CPI looks like this:

CONSUMER PRICE INDEX - TABLE OF DATA			
Item	Jun99	May99	Apr99
CPI	0.1	0.3	0.4
All items less food and energy	0.2	0.2	0.4
Food and beverage	0.1	0.1	0.7
Foods	0.1	0.1	0.7
Meats, poultry, fish, eggs	-0.2	0.0	-0.2
Fruits, vegetables	0.7	-0.2	5.1
Alcoholic beverages	0.1	0.3	0.3
Housing	0.2	0.1	0.3
Shelter	0.2	0.4	0.4
Fuel, utilities	0.4	-0.4	0.2
Household furnishings	-0.2	0.0	-0.1
Apparel and upkeep	0.4	0.4	0.7
New Cars	0.1	0.1	0.6
Used Cars	-1.1	-0.7	0.4
Medical Care	0.3	0.3	0.3
Entertainment	-0.2	0.5	0.3
Tobacco, smoking products	0.9	0.5	0.3
Energy	0.5	0.5	0.4
Compounded Annual Rates			
CPI	1.6	3.2	4.9
1999 year-to-date	3.2		
Core CPI	2.3	2.3	4.6
1999 year-to-date	3.6		

Once again, all of the numbers are percentages.

EMPLOYMENT

The various employment reports are all very highly scrutinized, because they go to the heart of what economic expansion is supposed to do, namely, give us jobs so we can feed our families. There are two main reports to be aware of in the employment area.

Every month the Labor Department releases a report on US employment. This employment report is composed of two parts. First is the report on non-farm payrolls, which is gathered using interviews with employers. This process of interviews is known as the establishment survey. The second part of the report is the unemployment rate report. This report is based on interviews with workers, a process known as the household survey.

The data release for the report looks much like the following table.

Total Employment and the Labor Force, Feb 2004						
Category	Quarterly Averages 2003		Monthly Data			Jan-Feb Change
	III	IV	2003 Dec	2004 Jan	Feb	
Household Survey	Labor Force Status (In thousands)					
Civilian labor force	146,628	146,986	146,878	146,863	146,471	-392
Employment	137,647	138,369	138,479	138,566	138,301	-265
Unemployment	8,981	8,616	8,398	8,297	8,170	-127
Not in labor force	74,885	75,290	75,631	75,298	75,886	588
	Unemployment Rates					
All workers	6.1	5.9	5.7	5.6	5.6	0.0
Adult men	5.8	5.5	5.3	5.1	5.1	.0
Adult women	5.2	5.1	5.1	5.0	4.9	-.1
Teenagers	17.5	16.3	16.1	16.7	16.6	-.1
White	5.4	5.1	5.0	4.9	4.9	.0
Black or African American	11.0	10.7	10.3	10.5	9.8	-.7
Hispanic or Latino ethnicity	7.8	7.1	6.6	7.3	7.4	.1
Establishment Survey	Employment (In thousands)					
Nonfarm employment	129,820	130,002	130,035	130,132	130,153	21
Goods-producing	21,718	21,676	21,668	21,688	21,663	-25
Construction	6,738	6,766	6,774	6,808	6,784	-24
Manufacturing	14,410	14,340	14,324	14,311	14,308	-3
Service-providing	108,102	108,326	108,367	108,444	108,490	46
Retail trade	14,912	14,915	14,876	14,936	14,949	13
Professional and business services	16,023	16,114	16,159	16,149	16,159	10
Education and health services	16,594	16,705	16,731	16,743	16,756	13
Leisure and hospitality	12,120	12,172	12,192	12,211	12,202	-9
Government	21,560	21,549	21,544	21,538	21,559	21
	Hours of Work					
Total private	33.6	33.7	33.6	33.8	33.8	0.0
Manufacturing	40.2	40.6	40.6	40.9	41.0	.1
Overtime	4.1	4.4	4.5	4.5	4.5	.0
	Indexes of aggregate weekly hours (2002=100)					
Total private	98.2	98.7	98.4	99.0	98.9	-0.1
	Earnings					
Average hourly earnings, total private	$15.41	$15.45	$15.45	$15.49	$15.52	$0.03
Average weekly earnings, total private	517.67	520.55	519.12	523.56	524.58	1.02

Non-Farm Payrolls

The name of this report is a bit misleading. The government doesn't dislike farmers, even though they do work outside in the hot sun, and get a bit, you know, smelly.

It's a historical holdover from earlier times when many more Americans were self-employed at farming than is the case today, and farming was the main source of self employment. Things are much different today, so what the report is really referring to is workers employed by businesses as employees. It includes all the working people in the country who do not work on farms, or are self-employed, proprietors, domestic workers, or volunteers.

This report enumerates all the new jobs that were created outside the farming sector of the economy. Every basic sector of the economy is listed, along with how many new jobs were created in each sector. This is a key report.

In a nicely booming economy, we should create about 200,000–300,000 new jobs a month. That's a nice growth rate, and it means your worthless brother-in-law may actually get a job. In recessionary times, of course, people can actually start losing jobs, and instead of new jobs being created, jobs may be eliminated. In non-recessionary times, US businesses create about 2 million new jobs a year.

The reason this report is so important is that it gives you a monthly snapshot at how fast new jobs are being created, which indicates how fast companies are expanding and new businesses are starting up. This report gives you an indirect look at the performance of the economy as a whole.

Besides telling you how many new jobs were created (or lost) the payroll number also has some other interesting information. The Labor Department also adds in the average hourly wages and the average workweek. The average hourly wage number is important because it can give you a snapshot of how inflation is affecting wages. If hourly wages start to climb, then consumer prices may head upwards, too. Wages and prices tend to mirror each other, so economists look very carefully at hourly wages for indications that rising wages may start causing prices to rise.

The relationship between rising wages and prices is called the wage-price spiral. As I've said before, rising prices are the result of too much money chasing too few goods. Well, rising wages can be called too much money chasing too few workers.

If the employment rate is very low, employers may need to push wages a bit higher to attract more employees. If wages go up enough, retailers may push prices up because they, after all, are paying more to their employees which makes doing business more expensive. This can begin a vicious wage-price spiral because now employees will want more money as prices rise and their paychecks are worth less in real terms. Before you know it, everybody is driving a $500,000 car and wearing $2,000 suits. So economists get very worried about the wage-price spiral. If it gets out of hand, horrible things can result as inflation rises.

In Brazil, inflation in the first part of 1995 was 920% per year! Imagine a country where there are no coin-operated vending machines because prices change every day, and so you can't program Coke machines to keep up with the rise in prices.

So inflation in wages is watched very carefully, because it is harder to control than inflation in prices. It also tends to be more permanent. Once employees receive a raise, it is sort of difficult to get them to take a pay cut later.

The general rule: inflation bad; price stability good.

The average weekly hours are an interesting part of this report, too. If workers are starting to work a lot of overtime—more than 40 hours a week—it may indicate the economy is expanding at a rate that keeps businesses hard pressed to keep up with it. Businesses may also be having a hard time finding workers. In that case, businesses may need to start raising pay to attract workers.

Oops! Wage inflation again. On the other hand, if the weekly hours worked keep falling, it means that businesses are below capacity, and people may need to be fired. Which means your worthless brother-in-law will probably be laid off again, and need another loan from you.

Unemployment Rate

In addition to the report on non-farm payrolls, the Labor Department's Unemployment report tells us how many people are in the workforce, how many are employed, how many are unemployed, and what the rate of unemployment is.

Pretty straightforward, right?

Unfortunately, it's not as straightforward as it looks. At the time of this writing, there is quite a bit of controversy going on about the employment report, because the figures in non-farm payrolls and the unemployment report don't quite add up.

In the year prior to the Employment report shown in the chart above, the establishment survey indicated that 122,000 jobs were created between February 2003 and February 2004. But, the household survey indicated that one million new jobs had been created over that same period.

That's a pretty big difference, and at the time of this writing, economists haven't figured out why. The establishment survey is more accurate than the household survey. But a difference of nearly 900,000 jobs is hard to dismiss as a relatively minor statistical error.

The household survey is telling us a story: Declining unemployment and moderate job creation. This is consistent with 4%+ rates of economic growth. The establishment survey is also telling us story: stagnant employment and productivity-fueled economic growth. This is consistent with 6%+ rises in productivity.

But these two stories are inconsistent, to say the least. Everything we know about the past, all of our experience, tells us that employment growth as measured by the establishment survey should be increasing as the economy expands.

This isn't an argument about the relative accuracy of two employment surveys. This is a serious question about why employment growth is not consistent with economic growth, according to the relationship we've known about for a couple of generations.

There are two possibilities:

1) The expected employment growth is taking place, and we are missing it because it is happening through self-employment and contract work. Unfortunately, we don't have statistics of sufficient reliability to pin this down with any accuracy. This implies, by the way, that our figures on productivity growth may be flawed, because we are low-balling the number of actual workers out there, meaning that our estimates of output per worker are incorrect.

2) The employment growth is not occurring, and our long-accepted understanding of the relationship between economic and employment growth is flawed. This means that something is seriously wrong with the household survey's estimate of unemployment, and that the rate of unemployment is substantially higher—on the order of one percentage point—than the household survey indicates. This also implies that if productivity keeps improving at the current rate, then sometime in the next 20 years, all US economic output will be produced by a single worker, resulting in an unemployment rate of approx. 99.9999999998%

Of course, some mixture of the two could also be going on.

One of the key economic arguments about this disparity between the two reports concerns the issue of self-employment. The establishment survey contacts businesses, and, as such, it misses the self employed entirely. Unfortunately, the household survey isn't much help, because all it does is ask respondents if they are employed. It doesn't ask them *how* they are employed. That means that you can't really do anything but "guesstimate" the number of self-employed people.

There are some secondary indicators you can look at. States, for example, release statistics on the number of Limited Liability Corporation (LLC) filings. This is a type of corporation filed by many self-employed people, like lawyers. In Illinois in 2003, 18,600 LLCs were created, a 45% jump over 2002. In that same year, Tennessee saw an increase of nearly 16%.

Obviously, increasing numbers of people were becoming self-employed over that period. As to whether it's enough to account for the discrepancy, no one knows, because we simply don't have any available statistics that can tell us.

Hopefully, in the future, economists can explain to us why they are so confused right now.

Weekly Claims for Unemployment

Another important employment number is the weekly report on initial unemployment claims. This report tallies how many people have signed up for unemployment benefits for the very first time in the last week. The weekly number is a bit volatile, though, so the important part of this report to look for is the four-week moving average. This is the average number of claims that have been filed each week for the last month.

A key number to remember here is 400,000. If there has been an average of 400,000 new claims each week for the past month, then that is indicative of a recession. A number below 400,000 indicates an economic expansion.

Also, in general, there are about 3 million people receiving unemployment benefits at any given time. Most of those people are only temporarily out of work and are moving between jobs.

JOBLESS CLAIMS - TABLE OF DATA				
WEEK ENDED	**JULY 22**	**JULY 15**	**JULY 8**	**YEAR AGO**
Adjusted Basis				
Initial claims	374,000	416,000	399,000	328,000
4 week average	389,000	387,750	382,750	355,250
Unadjusted basis				
Initial claims	411,641	491,112	428,632	354,495
Total receiving benefits	2,780,000	2,708,000	2,767,000	
% of covered jobs	2.5%	2.4%	2.6%	
Numbers are seasonally adjusted. Previous week's claims are revised				

Note the statement at the bottom. Many times, conditions will skew a series of economic numbers at certain times of the year. If the numbers aren't adjusted to account for this, they will be hard to understand. So the government uses "seasonal adjustment factors". Sometimes more claims will be filed because seasonal work ends. Summer jobs for college students, for example. But in the greater economy, nothing has changed. Seasonal adjustment factors take these discrepancies into account. That is why there is sometimes such a large difference between the adjusted and unadjusted claims. Go with the adjusted claims if you're going to quote the figures.

GENERAL BUSINESS CONDITIONS

The most important of these reports is the monthly survey released by the Institute for Supply Management[1]. Every month, the ISM surveys all of their members. The surveys are answered by the purchasing officers in every major manufacturing industry in the country. The reason this is so significant is that the purchasing officers are responsible for

---

1.   Formerly known as the National Association of Purchasing Managers (NAPM), their monthly survey was called the NAPM Report or the Purchasing Manager's Survey.

keeping raw materials coming in to their business. They know the rate at which they need materials, how much manufacturers are paying for raw materials, how many orders they have backlogged, and all sorts of stuff like that.

Purchasing managers are like the traffic cops in the production process; they keep the production process flowing along by pouring in the right amount of raw materials.

The ISM survey is a closely watched report. It reveals almost a complete picture of the county's manufacturing base: employment plans, wages, prices paid for materials, how long it takes to receive shipments, how large they are backed up with orders, how many new orders they are getting, and so on. In other words, the ISM is the whole shootin' match, and is generally the most important report of the week. It is always released on the first business day of the month.

On the last business day of the month, the Chicago area Association of Purchasing Managers releases the survey of purchasing managers in the Chicago area. This report is closely watched because the Chicago report often clues you in on what the national report will say. But not always. Take it with a grain of salt.

Previously, when we discussed the report on GDP, we discussed the concern with business inventories that was going on in 1995. The ISM Survey for July, 1995, was released a few days after the government released the GDP number. The ISM Survey confirmed many of the conclusions economists made after seeing the GDP report. The index rose above 50, and the new orders index shot up by ten points. This number also confirmed the view that the inventory correction was ending. Here is the ISM Survey for July, 1995:

NAPM Purchasing Manager's Survey - July, 1995			
Category	Jul 95	Jun 95	May 95
Purchasing Manager's Index	50.5	45.7	46.1
New Orders Index	53.3	*3.4	*3.2
Backlog	41.5	36.0	42.0
Production Index	50.9	44.8	48.5
Supplier Deliveries	50.4	51.2	52.9
Inventories	46.7	*3.9	42.7
Prices	58.3	65.6	711
Employment	47.7	46.9	*3.9
New Export Orders	57.9	56.7	55.8
Import Orders	54.2	48.9	46.5

The results of the ISM survey are expressed as a percentage of manufacturers reporting increases in a given area. For example, an overall reading of 50.5 for the Purchasing Manager's Index (PMI) indicates that 50.5% of manufacturers are reporting better business conditions. By reporting the numbers this way, a reading of 50 becomes essentially neutral. Any number below 50 indicates a general contraction of business and a reading above 50 indicates expansion.

As you can see above, the PMI moved back into slightly positive territory after two months of contraction. Even better, new orders jumped dramatically while the Prices Index fell below 60 for the first time in a long time. Just like the GDP report that was released a few days before this ISM survey, the weak overall number hid signs of growing strength.

Consumer Sentiment Report

Another important series are the reports on consumer sentiment. These reports are important not because they tell you anything specific, but because they can clue you in on the overall trend in the economy. But you have to read them very carefully. The US government has a consumer sentiment report, but the more carefully watched reports come from the Conference Board, a business think-tank in New York City, and the University of Michigan.

All of the reports do basically the same thing, though. They just show you whether consumers feel good or bad about the economy, their jobs, and their personal finances.

That's important, because people who think they're about to be fired, be unable to find a job because the economy's bad, and who have no personal savings tend not to go out and buy new stuff. On the other hand, people who think they've got a job for life and money to burn are out spending every free dime they have. Obviously, those two extremes are going to make the overall economy look different.

It's important to remember one thing about this series: just because consumers feel good about the economy doesn't mean the economy is fine, and vice versa. Most consumers don't know diddly about the economy, frankly, and don't care. What they know about is their own personal situation, and that colors their responses to the survey.

But their attitudes do tend to shape their buying habits, so you need to keep up with how consumers are feeling. Additionally, their attitudes, taken as whole, reflect, even if only in the most general fashion, in what direction the economy is moving. Consumers who don't feel confident don't spend money if they don't have to. And when the economy gets weak, consumers feel less confident.

Retail Sales

Retail sales are another key indicator. The Johnson-Redbook Retail Sales Report is a weekly look at a broad part of the retail sector. Every week, the boys and girls at Johnson-Redbook tally up how retailers did that week and compare it with sales the prior week, and during the same week the previous year.

This is a difficult series to follow, because sales can fluctuate so much from week to week, so you really need to get a look at four or five weeks of this report to tell how retail sales are doing. In general, you want sales to be up by about 5%–10% over last year. And small weekly rises are nice to see, too.

But, keep in mind that in some months, sales are *always* bad. January is a bad month, for example, because everybody's broke from Christmas spending. (Except for the kids. Those little rug rats are happy as clams. Unfortunately, they don't have any money, so they aren't buying either.) April's a bad month, too, because we've all gotta send taxes in to those government jerks at the IRS. On the other hand, June and July can be pretty good months, because our IRS refunds are back!

Every month, national reports on retail sales are also released by all the country's retailers. These are the actual sales reports, and they show exactly how all of the retailers did, company by company. Johnson-Redbook can give you a clue about how the actual retail sales report will look, but these are the actual numbers. This series can be a little hard to wade through, because every retailer reports their sales results individually.

Fortunately, the government weighs in on retail sales, too, but the government's numbers are split into the main sectors of the retail trade, so you can see how different sections of the retail community are doing at a glance. The government's numbers give you the macro view, while the retailers' reports give you the micro view.

RETAIL SALES - TABLE OF DATA				
% Change from previous month	Jun95	May95	Apr95	Mar95
Retail trade, total	**0.7**	**0.9**	**-0.1**	**0.7**
Total ex. auto group	0.3	0.5	0.2	0.4
Durable goods, total	**1.3**	**1.4**	**-0.6**	**1.1**
Building materials, hardware, garden, mobile homes	0.9	-1.3	-2.5	1.1
Automotive dealers	1.9	2.0	-0.8	1.6
Furniture, home furnishings	0.3	1.0	-0.5	-0.6
Non-durable goods, total	**0.3**	**0.6**	**0.3**	**0.4**
General merchandise group	1.0	0.7	0.0	0.4
Dept. stores (ex. leased)	1.1	0.5	1.1	0.0
Dept. stores (md. leased)	0.9	0.7	0.2	0.4
Food stores	-0.4	0.2	0.5	-0.5
Grocery	-0.4	0.4	0.5	-0.5
Gasoline service stations	0.7	0.7	-0.2	1.2
Apparel and accessory	0.3	2.9	-3.7	1.9
Eating and drinking	-0.2	0.3	1.1	0.8

Durable Goods Orders

The next important economic report is for durable goods. Durable goods are generally expensive items that last a few years. Cars are durable goods (Well, Japanese cars are, anyway). Refrigerators and microwaves are durable goods, too. So are jet fighter planes, tanks, aircraft carriers (although, if a war breaks out, they tend to become a lot less durable). Industrial machinery and jumbo jets are durable goods, too.

The reason we care about durable goods is that if people and businesses are ordering this type of good, it means that they are confident that they have the money to pay for them. People tend to cut way back on expenses in hard times, and companies do, too. So, this number can be a good gauge of both confidence, and investment in capital goods by businesses. If people are confident enough to buy durable goods, they're probably spending more in other areas of their lives. By the same token, if businesses are buying more capital goods and machinery, then productivity will probably rise and output will increase.

Durable Goods Orders - Table of Data			
Category	Jun95	May95	Apr95
New orders for durables (% change)	-0.1	2.6	-4.6
Excluding Defense	0.0	2.4	-3.5
Excluding Transportation	0.2	2.5	-2.8
Non-Defense capital goods	-0.6	7.6	-6.0
Defense capital goods	-1.4	7.4	-27.8
Transportation equipment	-1.8	2.9	-10.2
Machinery orders, excl. electrical	3.7	3.1	-4.8
Electrical machinery	-2.6	4.1	-3.2
Primary metals	2.3	-1.0	-3.7
Durable goods shipped	0.9	1.0	-2.2
Backlog of orders	-0.4	0.0	-0.6

NOTE: The category called excluding defense equals total new for durable goods minus defense-related orders. The category non-defense capital goods equals all orders for capital goods industrial machinery and computer and office equipment, minus related goods.

Federal Reserve Reports

The Fed puts out some economic reports on business conditions that should be taken seriously as well. The first series to look at is industrial production and capacity utilization. The Fed looks at these readings very carefully.

Industrial production is a report that tells you how much output is increasing or decreasing at US factories. The production index tells you how much industry is producing now compared with the base year of 1987. A reading of 100 on the production index indicates that production levels we equal to those of 1987.

Capacity utilization tells you what percentage of factory production is currently in use. The capacity utilization figure is especially important, because the Fed uses this as a key gauge of inflationary pressure.

Historically, when capacity utilization reaches 85% or thereabouts, the prices of goods start to rise. Once you reach the 85% point, factories have to hire more workers, more overtime has to be paid, and the rising price of producing goods begins to be passed on to the consumer. In other words, the 85% point is where the demand for goods begins to outstrip their supply. If the Capacity utilization figure starts to approach that magic 85% reading, the Fed will probably begin raising interest rates to cool the economy off, and keep prices stable.

Industrial Prod., Cap. util. - Table of Data	Jun95	May95	Apr95
Industrial production	0.1	-0.1	-0.7
Production index (100=1987)	121.0	120.9	121.1
Capacity Utilization (%)	83.5	83.7	84.1

Another important series of Fed reports are the business surveys conducted by some of the regional Federal Reserve Banks. They are designed to get a reading on general business conditions.

These surveys are carried out by asking business executives to rate their business conditions, employment plans, prices paid for materials, unfilled orders, new orders, the size of their inventories, and how many goods they're shipping. The most important of these surveys is probably the one conducted by the Federal Reserve Bank of Philadelphia, because it tends to be the most representative of nationwide business conditions. This survey is usually called the Philly Fed Survey. Most economists don't pay much attention to the other surveys, but the Atlanta Fed and Richmond Fed surveys are released every month, for those who care.

For the Philly Fed Survey, you just need to know that a reading of zero is neutral. A minus reading indicates that business conditions reflect a slowing of business, a positive reading shows that business is picking up. The Philly Fed business conditions index for March of 2004 was 24.2, indicating that business conditions were improving that month. At the same time, the previous month's reading was 31.4, so while Conditions were improving in March, they weren't improving as quickly as they had the previous month.

CONCLUSION

Whew! It's good to get those numbers out of the way!

Obviously, I've only shown you a few of the many economic numbers that are released each year. Actually, state and local authorities, combined with the federal government, release thousands of reports each year, but the ones I've presented are the main ones.

There is another class of economic statistics that are important, and those concern the statistics on international trade. But, to cover that subject properly, we will devote the next chapter to it.

For now, though, the numbers presented in this chapter should give you a fair idea of how the economy is doing. Once you are comfortable with them, you'll be able to speak as knowledgeably about the economy as almost any real economist.

And you'll be just as wrong as they are.

6

HEATHEN FOREIGNERS

THE CONCEPT OF TRADE

You see the names everywhere: Toshiba, Mitsubishi, Philips, and Mercedes. And even if you don't see the names, you see other signs. The tag in your T-shirt says "Hecho en Mexico". The stuffed toy you want to buy for your child has a tiny little "Made in China" tag. Everywhere you look, stores are full of foreign goods. Even when you go to the grocery store, even fruit has little "Product of Argentina" stickers plastered to it.

It's the work of foreigners, sold openly on our streets!

And it's, as Martha Stewart used to say, before her unfortunate run-in with the US Government, a Good Thing, too. Nations that engage in trade with one another end up richer than nations that limit trade.

It might be hard to believe that, given what you often hear on the news. The headlines scream, "Nation's Trade Deficit Worse Than Ever", or "US Firms Sending Jobs Overseas". In such an atmosphere, it might be hard for you to understand why trade between nations is good. You might even think that restricting trade would help improve the economy.

I would agree with you, but you're wrong.

The guy who first figured out why you're wrong lived 200 years ago, and his name was David Ricardo.

The Theory of Comparative Advantage

Ricardo was an English economist who lived from 1772 to 1823. He was one of the greatest of the early economists. His primary contribution to the field of economics came when he realized that different countries do some things better than others. In fact, after studying the subject, he came to the conclusion that even if one nation does *everything* better than every other country, it still helps everyone to engage in trade.

How could that possibly be?

Ricardo's explanation was that even if every country made good products, some countries would have a *comparative* advantage at making them over other countries. To prove his theory, he used the examples of port wine and wool.

Britain made lots of wool. There were sheep galore in England. Every farm had whole herds of them. Why they were practically the national animal. Even in the cold and barren Scottish Highlands, farmers kept sheep. Britain was practically the sheep capitol of the world.

It's probably not wise to ask why sheep were so popular with farmers, so let's just accept that they were.

Spain, on the other hand, also had sheep. And fine, silky sheep they were, too. But what Spain really had was a fine wine product called Port. Not only was it tasty, but it could get you liquored up real good. And the English, in addition to their sheep, really loved Port. In fact, it is said that drinking a lot of Port would sometimes intersect disturbingly with the love of sheep, but let's not go there.

The British could probably make Port. After all, British agriculture was the glory of the civilized world. The climate in Spain was warm and sunny, and was better for growing grapes but, in point of fact, Britain had far more arable land than Spain did. Even with a worse climate for growing grapes, the amount of land available for grape cultivation was far higher than that of Spain, so, in all probability, Port production in England would be higher than that of Spain.

Britain, on the other hand, being rather damp and gray, had produced magnificently wooly sheep. Spain's sheep, while, of course, handsomely furred, weren't quite as shaggy as the good old English sheep. Spain could produce wool, but it would take longer, or would require significantly more sheep to make the same amount of wool clothing, blankets, and what have you.

So, Ricardo wondered, if Britain could make both wool and Port, and make more of it than the Spaniards could, then why buy all that hooch from Spain? And, for that matter, since most of Spain was sunny and warm, why couldn't they produce their own woolen jackets? After all, they wouldn't even need as many of them, or make them as thick and warm. That way, England and Spain could both produce their own Port and wool, and they wouldn't have to trade with one another at all.

To answer that question, let's say the England can make both wool and Port wine better than Spain. In fact, let's say that, in the course of a week, England can produce 1000 bottles of Port or 2000 wool jackets. Spain, on the other hand, can only produce 500 bottles of Port or 1,000 wool jackets. Whether it's Port or wool, Britain can make more of it. Britain has an absolute advantage in both areas.

Now, let's assume that people get equal pleasure out of a tasty bottle of Port or a nice, snug jacket. If both Britain and Spain spend half their time making jackets and the other half making Port, then, at the end of the week, the results of their respective production will look like this:

Country	Jackets	Bottles of Port	Total Units
Britain	1000	500	1500
Spain	500	250	750
		Total Units	**2250**

But, what happens when Britain decides to concentrate on making jackets, and the Spanish stick to Port? In that case, the production totals look like this:

Country	Jackets	Bottles of Port	Total Units
Britain	2000	0	2000
Spain	0	500	500
		Total Units	**2500**

Spain has a comparative advantage in the making of Port wine, while Britain has a comparative advantage in the production of jackets. Even though Britain is better at making both products on an absolute basis, both countries can produce more if they concentrate on the areas in which they have comparative advantage, and simply trade with each other to get what they want.

And there's still enough Port for everybody to have wine-tasting parties with button-nosed coeds.

See, everybody wins.

Creative Destruction

One thing you should notice about this example though is something that is always at the heart of the argument on free trade. What happens to the poor English vineyard workers in England or the stout wool farmers in Spain if the two countries concentrate on other things?

The undeniable fact of free markets is that conditions for individual workers can be affected badly when market conditions change. Those workers may face some tough times while they are learning a new trade, and some individuals may never do as well as they did before the change took place.

At the turn of the century, when the car began to replace the horse as the primary mode of personal transportation, the same questions could have been asked. What ever will happen to the poor makers of saddles and buggy whips? How will the workers who clean horse poo off the streets find gainful employment?

The answer is that new discoveries and inventions create new jobs that didn't exist before. Instead of jobs making buggy whips, there were new jobs working on auto assembly lines, manufacturing engine parts, and making rubber tires. All of the old horse-based jobs rapidly disappeared. In their place, a far greater number of jobs were created in the automobile industry. In fact, the automobile boom encouraged booms in other industries. Because people could travel farther, there was a greater need for hotels and motels. The beginnings of a travel and tourism industry came into being.

No matter how tough things were for those people who had worked in the horse-based economy, huge numbers of new jobs were created in industries that barely existed in the horse and buggy days.

The economist Joseph Schumpeter (1883–1950) called this process "creative destruction", and it's a very necessary part of increasing the wealth of society as a whole.

The free market is an evolutionary, indeed, a revolutionary economic system. As Schumpeter put it[1]:

> The fundamental impulse that sets and keeps the capitalist engine in motion comes from the new consumers, goods, the new methods of production or transportation, the new markets, the new forms of industrial organization that capitalist enterprise creates.

Free-market capitalism consists almost entirely of evolutionary and revolutionary change. Every day new consumers, new producers, new products, new management methods, and a whole host of other things are added to the economy. Businesses constantly seek new services and products to sell to customers. Customers constantly seek to find products offered with better prices or better quality. New technologies create entire industries from scratch.

For a couple of years, I worked as an advisor and corporate expert for SAIC, the largest employee-owned corporation in the world. Every one of its 40,000 employees worked in industries and technologies that didn't even exist in 1970.

---

1.   *Capitalism, Socialism and Democracy*, New York: Harper, 1975, pp. 82–85:

Prior to the creation of the personal computer, the computer industry consisted of a relatively few computer experts, nearly all of whom worked in only the very largest corporations and universities. In the single decade of the 1980's, however, the computer industry exploded, and by the end of the decade, nearly every business, large or small, had at least one PC. By the end of the 1990s, the computer community had been transformed into a major industry, employing millions of Americans.

Of course, that process destroyed the jobs previously held by people at Sperry, Digital, and even IBM, all of whom were invested in making large mainframe computers and the software that ran them. Those people were forced to learn new skills to stay in the job market and stay competitive.

Some portion of them undoubtedly suffered significant hardship. Perhaps they were too old to invest in the time it took to learn an entirely new skill. Perhaps they were assembly line workers at the Digital plant in Albuquerque, New Mexico, who lost their jobs when the factory there closed.

But the end result of that massive explosion in computer technology was a huge number of new, high-paying, high-skilled jobs. The increases in productivity it brought about allowed us to buy a huge range of products less expensively. The net benefit to the creative destruction of the computer boom was a significant increase in wealth for all Americans. The children of those mainframe assembly line workers of the 1970s now have opportunities available to them that their parents could never dream of.

Trade and Labor

One of the benefits of free trade is that it acts as part of the force of creative destruction. Industries that are less productive, require fewer skills, or that are more labor intensive, are often best done by workers overseas. This creates room in the labor force for better-skilled and educated American workers to take up the higher-skilled jobs that are created as technology advances.

Fifty years ago, Americans made televisions and radios in domestic factories. Now, those industries have been almost entirely shipped overseas. Clothes were mainly produced domestically. Now that production is done overseas.

We could have "protected" all of those jobs by refusing to trade in TVs, clothes, or transistor radios with the rest of the world. The same is true for many other products, such as car parts, toys, and many other goods. But if we had done so, and millions of people were tied down doing those jobs, who would have worked in the new jobs created in nuclear medicine, travel and tourism, telecommunications, or software?

Many people would rather be computer programmers, cellular phone engineers, or MRI technicians rather than workers in a textile factory. But if the jobs required manufacturing TV sets, clothes or toys can never be sent overseas, how would they be able to do so? Every worker who is kept working on a transistor radio assembly line is one less worker who is available for employment as a cable television engineer, or free-lance web designer.

One must also remember that imports also create jobs, even as they may eliminate jobs elsewhere. The steel industry in the United States has shrunk due to competition from Japanese and Brazilian steel mills. As a result, many jobs in the US steel industry have disappeared.

At the same time, the availability of cheaper steel has meant that the makers of tractors or office furniture can now make their products more cheaply. That allows them to sell their products for a lower price, which increases demand, and hence production. Manufacturers of farm equipment or appliances are now more competitive, and can sell more products overseas. This has meant an increase in jobs for those companies in order to keep up with the increased demand. So, jobs weren't really lost, they were merely moved from one sector of the economy to another.

That means that workers in one sector of the economy might have to change jobs, but it doesn't mean that the number of available jobs shrinks as a result of trade.

In fact, quite the reverse appears to be true. Just as we export jobs to other countries, we import them as well. And it appears we import more jobs than we lose. At the time of this writing, the United States outsources $77.4 billion worth of jobs. At the same time, we have $131 being insourced[2]. That is a net benefit to the US of $53.6 billion worth of jobs coming to the US from overseas.

It is also important to remember that American workers aren't just drones who do nothing but work. They are consumers as well, who benefit from free trade. The availability of cheaper imports allows the consumer, who is, remember, also a worker, to buy a greater number of products than he could otherwise.

In 1965, a nice new RCA New Vista® color television started at $400. And those were 1965 dollars, not the weak puny little dollars we have today. The average worker took home around $100 per week. In other words, in terms of labor, a TV cost 120 hours of work to purchase.

Today, a 27-inch color TV with stereo sound can be purchased for $180. I know, because I just went to Wal-Mart's web site and checked the price. At the time of this writing—and you can confirm this by going back to the previous chapter—the average wage for an American worker is $15.52 per hour. That means that the cost of a nice color TV in terms of labor is now 11.6 hours.

Today's TV is larger, has a remote control, stereo sound, and is cable ready for hundreds of TV channels. And after buying it, the worker still has 108.4 hours of labor left to buy something else nice.

Free trade improves the life of American workers by increasing the value and range of goods that they can purchase.

---

2.   The *Wall Street Journal*, Monday, 15 Mar, 2004

One must also remember that free trade isn't just about imports; it's about exports as well. Each $1 billion in exports creates approximately 20,000 American jobs.

The Balance of Trade

One of the other criticisms one hears about free trade is that America always seems to suffer a trade deficit. This supposed to be a scary thing for some reason.

It is true that America imports far more than it exports. There are two measures of trade. The most commonly reported measure is the measure of merchandise trade. The merchandise trade report is released by the government each month, and it captures the value of trade in goods and services with the rest of the world.

US Merchandise Trade, Jan 2004 (In millions of dollars)				
	Category	Jan 04	Dec 03	Nov 03
Balance	Total	**-43,057**	**-42,692**	**-38,220**
	Goods	-48,392	47,921	-43,944
	Services	5,229	5,229	5,724
Exports	Total	**89,045**	**90,103**	**90,633**
	Goods	61,907	62,692	63,722
	Services	27,138	27,141	26,911
Imports	Total	**132,102**	**132,795**	**128,853**
	Goods	110,299	110,883	107,666
	Services	21,803	21,912	21,187

It's clear that, while we export more services than we import, we import a lot more foreign goods than we export US goods.

The picture doesn't improve when you look at the very broadest measure of trade, the Current Account. The Bureau of Economic Analysis releases the Current Account figures every quarter. The release contains the value of, well, *everything* that is traded. Foreigners buy airline tickets from US carriers, hotel rooms, and even more importantly, stocks and bonds. The current account tracks the complete financial picture of trade.

We're running a deficit there, too. For the 2003 calendar year 2003, the current account deficit increased by $61.0 billion to $541.8 billion. If you believe trade must be balanced, then you probably think that's a disaster.

But there's no particular reason why you should.

The current account deficit is skewed by one very important fact. The United States, and specifically the city of New York, is the financial capital of the world. No matter where you live in the world, if you want to invest in the largest, safest, and most stable market in the world, you have to buy US stocks and bonds. In essence, we import cash from overseas.

This means that foreign investors provide our businesses with cash through stock purchases. They underwrite our borrowing, both private and public, through bond purchases. The stability and reliability of US financial markets is a huge attraction to investors.

That influx of cash makes it possible for American companies to expand, and to send goods and services all over the world. It hard, therefore to argue that having a current account deficit is a bad thing in and of itself.

Why Free Trade?

We often talk of trade deficits as if "America" and "China" were trading with each other. But it is not "China" or "Japan" with whom we trade. Trade is conducted between individuals. Chinese, Japanese, and American consumers buy products, nations don't.

When seen in that context, it becomes clear that restrictions on trade are really nothing more than restrictions on the freedom of consumers to buy the products they want. Such restrictions limit the quantity of available merchandise, and raise the price as supply is diminished. That makes consumers poorer, not better off.

Protectionist arguments assume that if you place tariffs on foreign goods to "protect Americans from unfair competition" that those foreign companies bear the cost of those tariffs. But, of course, they don't.

Just as US businesses must pass on the cost of taxation to their customers, foreign companies must pass on the costs of tariffs to theirs. (A tariff, after all, is nothing more than a tax on imports.) In the end, it's American consumers who pay the costs of the tariff in the form of increased prices. The only people who benefit are the small number of Americans whose jobs are at risk. The price of that protection is higher prices and less wealth for all of their fellow Americans.

But wait, it gets worse. If the new tariffs raise costs for importers by enough, it prompts domestic producers to increase their prices as well. Let's say that an American-made business suit costs $200, and a suit made in Hong Kong costs $170. As people begin to by the foreign-made suit, American clothing makers lobby Washington for tariffs on the unfair competition from the "sweatshops" in Hong Kong, in order to save valuable American jobs.

Congress complies, and the next thing you know, there's a $50 tariff on suits made in Hong Kong. Those suits now cost consumers $220. US businesses, now protected by the tariff, can then safely raise their price to $220, due to the elimination of competition. "Hey," they think, "That's more profit for me!"

As a result, the price of a nice suit increases for everyone. Instead of consumers being able to buy a suit for $170, protectionism has now raised the minimum price to $220.

As this example shows, limiting free trade has negative effects on competition. One of the key strengths of the free market is that producers who can make something better or cheaper compete against producers who can't. Over time, this increases quality and reduces prices. The market eliminates bad businesses and rewards good ones. But without competition, there is less pressure on businesses to work faster or cheaper. Poor businessmen can stay in business longer. That's good for them, but not so good for consumers, who have limited choices and shoddy products.

In the late 1970s, Japanese car manufacturers began to enter the US Market, and sales took off. Japanese cars used much less fuel than

American cars, which was important in a new age of concern about fuel conservation. Japanese cars were cheaper than American cars, mainly because Japanese cars were smaller, and American cars tended to be huge, hulking mountains of steel. And—the ultimate insult—Japanese cars tended not to break down due to much stricter quality control.

For the first time, American car manufacturers faced competition from overseas. Their immediate response was not to improve quality, or introduce new lines to compete with Japanese cars. It was to fly straight to DC and ask for tariffs on imports.

That's not, by the way, a sign of confidence in your own products.

Fortunately, that didn't work, because we were trying to open Japan's markets as well. So, US automakers were forced to compete with Japanese cars. All the sudden, the people at Ford and GM became very interested in Japanese management and production techniques. To survive, they had to compete. That eventually meant, no more Chevy Citations, Ford Fairlanes[3], or Chrysler K-Cars. It meant reliable cars with features and economy the public was interested in buying. That's a good result for everyone.

Next, it's important to know that trade surpluses or deficits are neither good nor bad. Practically every American has a trade deficit with the local grocery store, Burger King, or dry cleaners. I don't know about you, but I've never sold anything to the 7-11 store down the street. For some reason, they just aren't interested in buying anything from me.

It's more important to ask *why* a country has a trade deficit, because it's the "why" that determines whether a trade deficit is bad, rather than the existence of the deficit itself.

For example, one country may have a trade deficit because the economy is growing so quickly and consumers have so much extra cash that

---

3.   In 1985, my USAF Security Police unit still had a 1980 Ford Fairlane as a squad car. One day, I took it out on a back road and timed it from 0 to 50 from a standing start. It took 48 seconds.

they require foreign goods, because they can't produce goods fast enough domestically.

Another country might have a trade deficit because the government is constantly inflating the currency. This makes goods from foreign countries relatively cheaper, which causes consumers to buy them instead of domestic goods.

In the first case, the trade deficit is a sign of a healthy, robust economy with demand so high that it's drawing in goods from all over the world. In the second case, the government is playing unwise games with the money supply, and the trade deficit is a sign that a stricter monetary policy needs to be implemented.

Either way, the existence of a trade deficit is economically neutral. The real issue is the underlying state of the economy. By the same token, our current account deficit is a sign of the fundamental strength and stability of American investments.

By the same token, a trade surplus isn't necessarily a sign that everything's peachy keen, either. Let's say we have a trade deficit—which to them is a huge surplus—with the tiny country of Kaplokistan. Kaplokistan is full of poor, benighted people who make $30 a year and they can't afford to buy anything from us except a pack of gum at Christmas, assuming they even *have* Christmas in that foreign hell-hole. We, on the other hand, find their droll little tribal carvings quite amusing. Since we can afford to buy all the carvings our hearts desire, and since they can only afford a relatively tiny shipment of Juicy Fruit, they end up with a huge trade surplus with us.

Wow. Maybe next year, they can buy a box of Velamints, too. Won't that be a party.

For Kaplokistan, a trade surplus is a sign that their economy sucks.

Finally, one often hears protectionists argue that other countries don't trade fairly with us. They impose tariffs, quotas, and other restrictions on free trade. If they don't trade fairly with us, why should we do so with them?

Framed that way, the question is an appeal to the good old American sense of fair play. But that isn't the real question. The real question is: If foreign governments reduce the selection and quality of goods available to their people, increase prices, and reduce productivity by eliminating competition, why shouldn't we?

Uh, because we're not morons.

Look, here's how it works in a lot of places. The general who runs the Army in Kaplokistan has a son who makes widgets. The army is a major investor in the kid's widget factory. An American widget maker wants to export widgets to Kaplokistan for a lower price. The president of Kaplokistan, in order to keep the army chief from starting a coup because the government didn't protect his kid's company, orders tariffs put on American widgets.

Well, you know, the people who end up getting hurt are the poor peasants of Kaplokistan, because the government wants to protect the general's son, the Widget King.

But that's no skin off *our* noses. If the Kaplokistanis want export their colorful little statues here, and our people want to buy them, then by all means, let them. There's no reason to punish our consumers because the Kaplokistani government is corrupt or incompetent.

The answer to trade restrictions in other countries is not to implement trade restrictions here, but rather to do the reverse: engage in unilateral free trade with them. At least that way, *our* consumers will have the widest possible selection of goods at the lowest price. No need for everybody to suffer.

The final protectionist objection to free trade is that, well, those foreigners, they run sweatshops that have *children working in them*! And they don't do enough to protect the environment! And their workers are poorly paid! Why, it's an outrage! High-paying American jobs at good wages are being sent off to be done by foreign children!

These people need a reality check.

If, in fact, 10-year old children in Myanmar can do these jobs, then why do we need to pay American adults an $18 per hour union wage—plus benefits—to do them? I mean, how much skill do these jobs actually require? It seems to me that your concern isn't so much for the children performing these jobs in Vietnam, as it is to convince your fellow Americans to keep paying you $18 bucks an hour with full medical benefits.

That aside, I do agree that, by our standards, having a 10-year old kid on a factory floor is icky. The poor little tyke should be in school. The trouble is that, even if we forced the government of Myanmar to stop allowing child labor, he still wouldn't be in school. He'd just be poor, broke, and hungry.

As difficult as it is for us to understand it, conditions in many countries in Asia and Africa are abysmal. People must live on as little as a few hundred dollars *per year*. Life for that child on a factory floor, making even the small amount of money he makes is infinitely preferable to wading through piles of trash in the city dump, looking for food.

Every time there's a factory opening in these countries, literally thousands of applicants line up in the street for 40 or 50 job openings. Evidently, they don't think these jobs are so bad, especially if it means living on $1,000 per year while the rest of the country lives on $300.

We can afford stringent environmental laws, and child workplace laws, and the whole raft of regulations that go with them, because even the very poorest Americans are, by the standards of much of the world, fantastically wealthy.

Countries such as the Sudan, Mozambique, Ghana, the Philippines and Vietnam are dirt poor. If we wish them to clean up their environments, have high workplace health and safety regulations, and all the other life-easing conveniences that we enjoy, then we have to help them to become as rich as we are.

In a very real sense, arguments such as these are nothing more than arguments to keep those places mired in poverty and disease for the foreseeable future. Advocates for the environment or for "living wages" in those countries are effectively arguing against any development there, since implementing there requirements would make such development uneconomical. Such people may call themselves "worker's advocates" but they are really advocates of poverty, starvation, and death for those countries who can't afford the luxuries we have in the West.

Dressing it up in the language of human rights and dignity doesn't make it any less unconscionable.

TRADE AND CURRENCIES

Here's the thing about trade: It's all about money. In more ways than you can imagine. To understand the effects that trade has on the world's economy, you have to understand a bit more about money, how it flows from one country to another, and what happens to it along the way.

The FOREX Market

For the most part, every currency in the world is freely traded back and forth in the Foreign Exchange, or FOREX market. Every day, traders use Japanese Yen to buy US Dollars, or British pounds to buy Argentine Escudos. The high point of the day is when the Vietnamese traders come in to flash their dongs at the market.

(Note to Vietnam: If you ever expect to be anything other than a juvenile penis joke in the world of international finance, then you have to call your currency something other than the "dong". Really. I mean it.)

The FOREX market is huge, and it keeps getting bigger every day. The primary reason to have the FOREX market is because that is how trade accounts get settled between countries.

If you own a German company that makes audiophile stereo equipment that is sold in America, then you have to have a way to exchange dollars for euros. Your product is made in Germany, and it is priced in euros. But Americans don't have any euros. So, when an American wants to buy your stereo, you give him a dollar price.

If you sell a radio for €100, and one euro is worth one dollar, then the dollar price of the radio is $100. If the Euro is worth $1.06, then the price of your radio in dollars is $106. Whatever the exchange rate is, you have to charge a dollar price that gets you €100.

When the American pays his $100 or so, your bank exchanges that money through the FOREX market, and you get a check for €100.

Because the currencies in the FOREX market flow freely, the exchange rates between any two given currencies are constantly changing on a minute-by-minute basis. Over the long term, trade imbalances will tend to increase or decrease a currency's value when compared to other currencies.

Let's say that the Euro-zone countries run a trade deficit with America, and the exchange rate for dollars and euros is 1:1. In the FOREX market, this means that Europeans are constantly selling dollars in order to buy Euros, but Americans aren't doing the reverse as much. This means that the demand for Euros rises while the demand for the dollar falls. This change in demand increases the price of euros relative to the dollar to 1.1:1.

So, now if you charge $100 for your stereo equipment, instead of €100, you only get €90. In order to keep making €100, you have to raise the price to your American customers to $110.

As a result, fewer Americans buy your product, and your exports decline. Because you aren't exporting as much to America, your trade surplus declines.

In this sense, trade imbalances are somewhat self-correcting. If you run a trade deficit with another country, the price of that country's currency will tend to rise, making its products more expensive, which lowers demand for them. This has some interesting economic effects over time, as the Japanese experience of importing to America has shown.

Japan, since WWII, has been primarily an exporting country, and exports have led Japan's economic growth. In the late 1940s through the 1960s, Japanese imports were considered a bare step above junk. By the end of the 60s, though, Japan had made huge strides in quality improvement. In addition, Japan began adopting a number of modern management practices that originated in the new thinking that was going on in America, but was slow to catch on here, mainly because of arrogance.

By the 1970s, helped along by the oil crisis, Japanese cars began to trickle, then to flood into the country. This meant that the Japanese had huge amounts of American dollars that needed to be converted into Japanese yen. So, the price of the Japanese Yen began to increase relative to the price of the dollar.

This set off warning bells in Japan, because so much of Japan's economic performance was tied to exporting goods. If the price of the yen rose too high in the FOREX market, Japanese cars sold in America would become more expensive. That would reduce sales, and harm the Japanese economy.

So, by the 1980s, in an attempt to keep the exchange rate reasonable, the Japanese began keeping those dollars in America instead of repatriating them to Japan. They began buying American landmark real estate properties, golf courses, and everything else they could get their hands on.

I remember the talk of the time was all about how the Japanese were taking over the world, and what master businessmen they were, and how America was in decline, Japan Inc., etc., etc., etc.

But the Japanese had a serious problem. That money couldn't all stay in America. They did, after all, have to pay the bills back home. And, as they repatriated that money, the Yen became worth more and more.

Then, the Japanese got another shock. At the beginning of the 1990s, recession hit, and real estate prices, among other things, collapsed. The Japanese, who had paid top dollar to Americans for all these flagship properties, got hosed. Americans then kindly repurchased those properties from the Japanese for pennies on the dollar.

As the nineties continued, and the exchange rate still kept climbing, the Japanese began creating American subsidiaries. Those subsidiaries have spent the 90's building assembly factories in the US.

The history of Japanese trade with the US, despite constant trade deficits, hysterical warnings of Japanese takeover of our economy, shrieks of vital auto jobs going to Japan, and all the rest, has essentially been the following story: We got lots of good cheap stuff from them, took their money, screwed 'em over in real estate deals, then took their auto assembly jobs as they exported them to America.

Nice doin' business with you boys from *Nippon*. Ya'll come back real soon, ya' hear?

Currently, the largest trade deficit the US has is with China. Unlike the Japanese yen, however, the Chinese renminbi is not declining in value. The reason is that the Chinese appear to be holding their dollars in cash rather than trying to convert them. Because China's economy is so export-driven, a rise in the value of the currency would hurt their economy by reducing exports. So, instead of converting dollars to renminbi and taking their profits, the Chinese appear to be holding on to their dollars to keep the renminbi low.

But, as the Japanese found out, I expect the Chinese will learn that you can't do this forever.

The Dollar: The World's Reserve Currency

The dollar is not like other currencies. The dollar is, and has been for decades, the world's reserve currency. Whenever investors get nervous about the baht or the ringgit, they buy dollars. Whenever things get sticky in Southeast Asia, no one wants to just stand around holding his dong. (Note to Vietnam: See what I mean? Please, stop me!)

The dollar is the only currency in the world that has a large enough supply, as well as the requisite economic and political stability, to serve as the "safe harbor" among currencies. There are, in fact, some countries that don't even control their own monetary policy any more because they either use US dollars as their official currency, or they explicitly tie the value of their currency to the US dollar.

This has some positive and some negative affects when it comes to trade.

On the positive side, of course, is that it makes the US an attractive nation for investment. On the down, side, however, it can make the value of US currency rather volatile at times.

For many currencies in the world, the only people who are using them, outside the citizens of a particular country, are those who are trading or investing in the country. No one keeps a hoard of, say, Brazilian reals for a rainy day.

For those who are trading and investing with other countries, they not only have to face the regular business risks that all investors everywhere have to face. They have additional risks peculiar to international trade.

First is political risk. Many countries have…uh…a spotty history of peaceful political change. There's always some general or admiral, or commie revolutionary who is obsessed with becoming President for Life. The fact that may mean shortening the life of the current President for Life and his cronies seems not to bother them overmuch.

And, of course, every time there's a new government installed, all the foreigners are thrown out for colluding in the corruption of the previous administration. That just won't be tolerated any more, no sir, you betcha, in the new and improved Republic of Kaplokistan.

So, there's always the chance that you could wake up one morning, and find out that years of investment have just gone poof, because the new leadership of Kaplokistan has nationalized your investment for the enrichment of the people. (Not, of course, to line the pockets of the new president. That would be wrong.)

But it really doesn't matter whose pockets are getting lined, 'cause it's a sure bet yours won't be.

On top of that, there's the currency risk. Everything you invest in Kaplokistan has to be converted into Kaplokistani plokis. To get your money back out, you'll have to convert your plokis to dollars. If the price of the ploki collapses, you're screwed. If the price of the ploki drops from 10 to 20 plokis to the dollar, then half of your money has just gone "poof". You have to depend on the government of the current President for Life to do the right thing as far as monetary policy goes.

So, foreign investment is risky in ways that domestic investment is not.

Unless, of course, you live in Kaplokistan.

Of course, central bankers all around the world know about political risk and currency risk. To protect the value of their nation's currency they bank away a variety of assets, including big stacks of US C-notes. At any given time, a country may have a couple billion in US currency just sitting around in a vault. Even Iraq's former dictator, Saddam Hussein, had nearly a billion stashed away, and we hadn't done any business with him for years.

The purpose of this money is not, as you might suppose, to have a little parting gift if the government is overthrown and officials have to flee to Bermuda. Sure, it comes in *handy* for that if it becomes necessary, but the real reason they use it is to protect their currency.

Developing countries often wish to have foreign investment to do a variety of things that they can't do for themselves yet. They may desire to have foreign developers build office buildings and factories, or general contractors to build roads and bridges. Foreign companies supply the financing and management expertise, and the locals can provide the labor. This means that investors at the very least often have to take currency risk in investing in the country, even if the government is stable.

For example, an American real estate management company that builds an office building won't be able to demand dollars in rent payments. They have to accept the local currency, and convert it to dollars when they repatriate the money. If the value of the local currency falls, they may begin to lose money. Not only will they seek to limit their own losses by getting out of their investment if they can, other potential investors will be scared away from investing there.

So, the central bank of that country will hold dollars, in order to intervene in currency markets if necessary. Sometimes, currency traders will pick a currency as a bad risk and begin unloading it, driving the value down. By holding a reserve of US currency, the National Bank of Kaplokistan can instruct its agents to enter the FOREX market and begin buying up all the plokis it can with the US dollars the bank holds in reserve. If the bank acts quickly and forcefully enough, it can stem the tide against the ploki, and prevent its value from being driven down to the point where it becomes less feasible to invest there for foreigners.

This has the added advantage of convincing foreign investors that the central bank has a firm commitment to maintaining the stability of the ploki. It reassures them that the country's financial authorities will work with them to maintain the best investment environment that it can.

This doesn't always work, unfortunately.

In 1997, a currency crisis was sparked in Asia. The crisis began in Thailand. Prior to that time, the Thai currency, the baht, was tied to the value of the US dollar. The Thai government decided to unpeg the baht from the dollar, and allow it float freely in the FOREX market.

Currency traders immediately began dumping the baht. There were several reasons for this. Because the dollar had increased in value during previous years, it was generally thought that the baht was overvalued. In addition, Thailand had been suffering from increased pressure from export competition with China. Also, some of Thailand's financial institutions were a bit...uh...shady, and they began to fail, which uncovered the fact that some shenanigans had been going on, often with the knowledge, if not the active participation of certain highly placed government officials. Finally, the county's economic growth had started to slow.

In fact, currency traders had tried to pound the Baht a few times prior to this, and the Bank of Thailand jumped in with dollars to hold up the baht's value. Eventually, though, the bank ran out of dollars and they had no choice but to let the baht float freely.

The FOREX market hammered it.

Then speculators began to take a look at other countries in the region. Maybe they had the same sort of problems as Thailand. Investors started getting edgy, and pulling out their money.

The fact was that Thailand's problems were pretty much confined to Thailand. But, once the panic started on the baht, pretty soon the currencies of Indonesia, The Philippines and Malaysia started coming under pressure. Before too long, the problem had spread even to countries that had stable economies and fairly transparent markets, like Hong Kong, Singapore, and Taiwan. Then, the parade was off to South Korea.

In the end, the crisis significantly hampered growth in Asia. And it even had effects in the rest of the world, too, as exports to Asian countries dried up. It's estimated that US GDP growth suffered a 0.4% drop as a result of the crisis.

The FOREX market is *huge*, and if a little country gets targeted by the traders, its central bank's dollar reserves might not do anything more than delay the inevitable.

CONCLUSION

Free trade is the best system yet devised for increasing the wealth, and raising the living standards of the whole world. Additionally by making everyone collectively richer, it allows developing countries to begin setting and enforcing standards of workplace safety and environmental protection.

It is no accident that workers in the West are the healthiest, covered by the most sophisticated health care, enjoy the safest workplaces, and live in the cleanest environments on earth. We enjoy those benefits because we are wealthy enough to do so, and a substantial portion of that wealth comes from trade.

If we wish to extend these advantages to the rest of mankind, then quickest way to do so is to ensure that they can become as wealthy as we are by trading with them.

7

POLITICAL ECONOMY

IT'S ALL POLITICAL

People are economic animals. It is not, to be sure, *all* that we are, but it is an integral part of our makeup. People are also political animals. As Carl Sagan once put it, we are all primates, and thus prone to dominance hierarchies. We organize ourselves into groups. We sort ourselves into leaders and followers. And we seek the most gain we can for our loved ones and ourselves.

As a practical matter, that means that there is a large area of our lives where politics and economics intersect. This intersection can often be full of raucous debate over policies that affect labor, money, and the economy.

In a sense, there are two branches of economics. Positive economics is the scientific portion. It looks at the choices people make in response to scarcity, and it defines the costs and benefits of our choices. Normative economics is the political portion. It is less concerned with what is, and more concerned with what *should be*. It is this tension that lies at the center of many arguments in the political economy.

Positive economics can tell us, for example what will happen when we implement a new minimum wage. If we need to know whether a minimum wage will decrease employment, positive economics can tell us.

Normative economics, however, is not a science. It doesn't seek to answer empirical questions, but questions of value. It is more akin to faith than reason. A normative question would be, "Knowing that a minimum wage tends to reduce employment among the poor, *should* we have a minimum wage?" There is no right or wrong answer to that question, except that which our own values give us.

In this final chapter, we will look at some political/economic issues, and try to provide the answers that positive economics can provide for us.

Answers to the normative questions, you'll have to answer for yourself.

THE MINIMUM WAGE

This is one of the most contentious economic issues of national scope in existence. Every few years a debate is sparked about whether or not to increase the minimum wage. In recent years, the idea of a minimum wage has begun to be eclipsed by the new argument that businesses have a responsibility to provide to their employees not just a minimum wage, but a "living wage", i.e., a wage at which it is possible to support a family.

The economic community has studies this issue for the last 50 years in the United States and come to a fairly universal consensus:

1) Increases in the minimum wage tend to reduce the number of minimum wage jobs.

2) The effect of the unemployment tends to fall mainly on the poor and/or minority worker

3) The chief beneficiaries of minimum wage legislation are middle-class persons who are:

    a) Not the primary breadwinner of the family

    b) The primary breadwinner working a second job

    c) Teenagers

This is not to say that the idea of a minimum wage is *always* wrong. As long as the wage is set sufficiently low to ensure that it doesn't distort the price mechanism by raising the cost of labor to a rate that is higher than the average worker's productivity, minimum wages are mostly harmless. I say mostly harmless because once you have a minimum wage, the pressure to keep on increasing it seems unstoppable over time.

The results we've seen in the US, for instance, seem to indicate that we have tended to set the minimum wage a bit too high. Results in Europe seem to indicate they've set it *way* too high. There is, after all a reason that 10% of Europeans are unemployed at any given time, or as in Holland, 14% of the workforce is on "disability".

Evidently Holland, a gentle land of rolling hills, meadows, and moderate weather, is just a fantastically dangerous place to work. I lived there for three years without so much as stubbing my toe, so I must be one of the luckiest men alive.

We tend to view employment in a different category than selling a good or service. But employment is an economic transaction, just like any other. The worker is selling his labor to a purchaser, the employer. The seller of labor wants to get the highest price he can. The buyer of labor wants to get the lowest price he can. Unless both the buyer and seller can come to a mutually satisfactory agreement on the price of labor, i.e., the wage, they can't make an agreement.

In a world of perfect competition, the prospective employee and employer would negotiate a wage, and both parties would negotiate on an equal footing. In the real world, the pressures faced by the employer and employees are different.

The employer must buy someone's labor. However, he is usually not under a great pressure from time. Until he can find an acceptable worker, he can have other workers put in a few extra hours. Alternatively, he can put off expanding his operations for a while. Additionally, there is usually a larger number of potential employees than there are available jobs.

The prospective employee may be under a much more pressing need. If he does not already have a job, he faces time pressures in the form of bills, rent or mortgage payments, car payments, etc. He has, therefore, an incentive to demand less than he might otherwise wish, as long as he receives a wage that lets him meet his obligations.

This is not, of course universally true. The prospective worker may still have a job, and simply be shopping around to sell his labor at a better price. If he doesn't get such a job in the short term, he still has adequate means to meet his obligation. In this case, the employer might be under more pressure to hire than the prospective employee is to *be* hired.

In the main however, at the minimum wage level of the job market, the former is far more often true than the latter. As a result, there are no negotiations for wages. The employer has a set wage, and the prospective employee decides whether or not to take the job at that wage.

No matter whom he hires, the employer must ensure that the worker can produce more in one hour than he is paid. If a worker can only produce $3 worth of product every hour, and he must be paid $5 per hour, this is an uneconomic transaction for the employer. If an employer must pay his workers $5 per hour, then each employee must produce more than $5 an hour worth of product. If they do not, the business will fail because it cannot operate at a loss.

In a free labor market, employees would be paid based upon the value of their productivity. An employee who produced only $3 worth of product per hour might be paid $2. A worker who produced $7 per hour might be paid $6.

As a practical matter, however, outside the garment industry and a few others where work can be done at piecework rates, i.e., a fixed rate for each item of production, or sales commission, few industries can do this. If an assembly line worker is part of a team that produces 100 computer keyboards every day, it's hard to bifurcate out individual wages based on production. Wages must be set at an average based on the unit's production as a whole.

Implementing a minimum wage puts a floor on the rate an employer must pay. It is a legal requirement that has no bearing whatever on the productivity of the workforce. Remember, a minimum wage increase raises the cost of labor. It doesn't make your employees smarter, or help them work faster. All it does is make labor more expensive to the employer.

As soon as a minimum wage is implemented or raised, employers have only two options if they wish to stay in business. They must either pass on the increased cost of labor to their customers, or they must lower their labor costs.

Trying to pass along price increases to customers is always a tricky business. As the price of a product increases, the demand for the product decreases. Consumers begin to look for substitutes, or to limit or eliminate their purchases of it. This lower demand translates into lower sales. In turn, lower sales mean that production must be reduced. If production must be reduced, then you really don't need to have all those people working on your production line.

On the other hand, you can skip right past all the tedious mucking around with customers and simply whack a few employees right up front. It gets you to the same place, but you don't have to risk your relationship with customers, or permanently reduce demand for your product by raising prices.

Either way, somebody's out of a job.

If you still need someone to fill those positions, you are still better off if you fire your least productive employees, and replace them with someone who is more productive. For example, you could dump that high-school dropout, and replace him with a college sophomore who's working his way through business school. That way your work force becomes more productive.

A more productive workforce reduces your labor cost by increasing the amount you produce without increasing your employment cost.

Notice what has happened here. In the worst case, you've had to eliminate jobs. In the best case, where you are able to maintain the same level of employment, you replace lower-skilled workers with more productive ones. As a result, minimum wage laws disproportionately harm poor and minority workers. White and middle-class workers are given an extra little bit of help, because they are generally possessed of better educations and job skills.

In this way, rather than being a help to the poor by increasing their wages, the minimum wage actually reduces their chances to be employed at all. A look at the unemployment rates of the lowest quintile of American workers tends to bear this out.

Prior to the implementation of minimum wage laws, poor workers were employed at about the same rate as other workers in the economy. Although a minimum wage was implemented in the 1930s, WWII and the rising wages that accompanied it essentially canceled it out. In the late 1940s, however, as minimum wage increases began to be passed, unemployment among the poor started to rise. Currently, nearly half of the households in the poorest 10% of the US population have *no one working at all*. If you don't have a job, it's hard to see how an increase in the minimum wage helps you.

There are about 5 million or so minimum wage workers in the country. At the same time, there are about 9 million people receiving unemployment assistance. Of those minimum wage workers, most of them are below 25 years old, and are students and secondary income earners. Advocates of increases in the minimum wage often try to paint a picture of minimum wage workers as the heads of households, but this is largely untrue.

Despite the above, there are still pockets of support, even in the economic community, for generous minimum wages.

A few years ago, two Princeton economists, David Card and Alan Krueger, released a study[1]. It purported to show that when the minimum wage was increased in New Jersey, it had no effect on minimum wage workers in the fast food industry. Quite the opposite, in fact. Employment appeared to have increased. From there, it became a short jump to arguing that increasing the minimum wage was a benefit!

---

1.   Card, D. E. & Krueger, A.B. (1995). *Myth and Measurement: The New Economics of the Minimum Wage.* Princeton: Princeton University Press.

Now, it doesn't really matter if you know anything about economics. All you have to do is ask yourself the question, "if someone raises the price of something, will they sell more of it, or less?" It's possible for a variety of reasons that Card and Krueger could be right, but the apparent violation of common sense should at least raise red flags.

Sure, it could be that New Jersey was having a fantastic economic rebound at the time of the study. That might have made labor scarce, causing employers to bid up the price for it. In that case, maybe increasing the minimum wage didn't raise it above the price employers were already paying. Sure, when the economy in New Jersey goes into recession, the bill for those extra labor costs will come due. But in the meantime, everything looks peachy. So it's possible that Card and Krueger were perfectly correct in their *results*, it was just their interpretation that was faulty.

Still, when other economists saw this study, some red flags went up. Economists, after all, know a few things about economics.

First, the study defied the vast majority of study results in this area. Most empirical studies simply disagreed with Card and Krueger's results. When Studies A through Y show one result, and study Z shows another, your first response isn't to go, "Hmm. I wonder what was wrong with those other 25 studies?"

Second, it defied common sense. Don't undersell common sense. It's a vitally important tool. If you see a study result that doesn't seem to make sense, well, maybe it doesn't. At the very least, it indicates you should look into the matter some more.

Finally, economists know that Card and Krueger have a well-known point of view about the minimum wage, especially David Card. Somehow, they always seem to find the minimum wage is of great benefit to everyone, employees and employers alike. In fact, had these two gentlemen come up with different results than the ones they published, *that* would have been a real surprise.

Economists also know that trying to replicate their results can be, uh, difficult. So, the economics community immediately tried to confirm their results. As it happens, Card and Krueger had based their results on telephone surveys with fast-food restaurant owners. To check up on the accuracy of such results, their critics went straight to the state's employment records.

It seems that Card and Krueger's survey respondents were misremembering. Or something. In any event, it seems their results didn't match up with the state of New Jersey's actual employment records. In fact, a rise in the minimum wage did appear to have decreased employment.

Few were surprised.

To this day, though, left-leaning policy groups quote this study incessantly, though, as well as Card's other work. And, really, they have to. These results are about all the left has when arguing for minimum wage hikes. As the Joint Economic Committee of the US House of Representatives[2] put it:

> While it is not yet clear why Card, Katz and Krueger got the results that they did, it is clear that their findings are directly contrary to virtually every empirical study ever done on the minimum wage. These studies were exhaustively surveyed by the Minimum Wage Study Commission, which concluded that a 10% increase in the minimum wage reduced teenage employment by 1% to 3%.

So, you know, you gotta wonder.

Finally, just ask yourself a simple question: If raising the minimum wage makes people better off, why not raise it to $500 per hour? Then, undoubtedly, we'd all be rich.

Wouldn't we?

INCOME DISTRIBUTION

In both domestic and international affairs, the issue of income distribution, or the inequality of wealth, is an increasingly hot topic.

---

2.   *50 Years of Research on the Minimum Wage*, 15 February, 1995

Even the term income distribution is a loaded one. As pointed out earlier, there is no central committee for distributing income. The method by which income is distributed is through the results of millions of people making voluntary decisions to buy and sell goods and services.

The rich, we are told, are getting richer while the poor get poorer. Often, advocates point to the figures showing declining household income. Oddly enough, they don't mention that the household size has been shrinking steadily from 4.5 people to about 2 people per household. Household income is shrinking because households are shrinking. Per-capita income, i.e., income per person, has been constantly *increasing*.

Still, we are told, wealth disparities are a serious problem. The obvious solution for those who worry about such things is to take wealth from the rich and redistribute it to the poor.

It's useless to point out that one of the major powers of the 20th century already tried that idea. The fact that the USSR is gone and Russia is now a fairly nasty place seems to make no impact on the redistributionists.

But it should, because the idea behind the redistribution of income is built on a lie. And it's a lie on more than one level.

First the foundation of the argument is false, because it's based on the proposition that economics is a zero-sum game: If I have too many brownies, you only get to lick the plate. But there is no fixed amount of wealth. If I have a boat, and you don't, it doesn't mean I took your boat. We can always build more boats.

Similarly, we can always produce more wealth.

Actually, it appears that we do. Despite the disparities between the rich and poor, we seem to have a little trouble defining who the members of these groups actually are. In reality, they are often the same people at different times in their lives. Between 1975 and 1993, an absolute majority of the people who were in the bottom quintile of income had moved into the top quintile[3]. Less than 3% of the people in the bottom quintile in 1975 were still there in 1993.

An even more telling statistic is the fact that people in the top quintile in 1993 worked an average of 52 hours per week. In the bottom quintile, 25% of the people didn't even have a full-time job.

Wealth is a function of productivity. For the most part, the reason people become rich in America is because they have produced goods and services. To the extent that people remain poor, it is because they don't.

The answer is not to redistribute the income of the rich, but to make the poor more productive.

The second lie is that to assume that we should all be equal. Now equality is a fine proposition, and it certainly works well as a working method when we step into the ballot box, or into a courtroom. It just doesn't work in real life. We don't all contribute equal value to society.

Let's take two gentlemen, Bill and Bob.

Bill drops out of college to start a small software company. Twenty years later, Bill's company makes the most popular office software in the world, along with a computer operating system used by almost 90% of all computers, everywhere. As a result, tens of thousands of people are employed at Bill's company. In addition, millions of people all around the world are employed in a vast software community, making databases and custom applications for businesses. The business community employs thousands of more people who all work with the same computer products, and who can always be sure that, when they send a file from New York to Seattle, the recipients will be able to open the file and read it instantly.

Bill becomes one of the world's richest men.

Bob, on the other hand, not only finishes college, but goes on to receive a master's degree in psychology with an emphasis on therapeutic counseling. He then goes to work in a drug rehab program in Los Angeles. At the end of 20 years, Bob has helped 5,000 people quit

---

3.   *Annual Report of the Federal Reserve Bank of Dallas*, 1995

drugs and assume productive lives. Bob is not rich, but receives the comfortable middle-class salary of a mid-level government employee.

Bill wanted to make some money. Bob wanted to help people. Bob's goals are certainly nobler than Bill's. But, in the end, whose work has been of more benefit to society?

Bill led a computer revolution that changed the world, employed millions and created vast amounts of wealth, both for him and millions of others, in an industry that barely even existed when he began. Bob may have been a nicer, kinder, person, and he's certainly helped a lot of people in important and fundamental ways. But there's no comparison between the advantages each man has bequeathed to society as a whole.

Equality, as a practical matter, doesn't exist anywhere, and never has.

Finally, the third lie inherent in the redistribution argument is that the argument itself is factually incorrect. The rich are certainly getting richer, but the poor are getting richer, too.

Currently, one of the major health problems among America's poor is obesity. This is a fundamentally different health problem than those associated with poverty in the past, like scurvy, or rickets.

In international affairs, a variety of advocates argue that America consumes a quarter of the world's resources, yet contains less than 5% of the world's population. Africans starve to death every day, while Americans worry about the super size of their Happy Meals. Americans, we are told, consume so much that there is nothing left for Africa.

America, with only 4.7% of the world's population, produces 31.2% of the world's GDP. America is the source of 40.6% of the world's R&D spending, one of the key predictors of future economic success. As *The Economist* puts it, "America again leads the world in all dimensions of power-military, economic, cultural, scientific—by a margin out of all proportion to its population." As the editors of the magazine put in one of their leaders[4]:

---

4.   *The Economist*, Mar 11th 2004, "A Question of Justice?"

But goods and services are not just lying around waiting to be grabbed by the greediest or most muscular countries. Market economics is not a zero-sum game. America consumes $10 trillion worth of goods and services each year because it *produces* (not counting the current-account deficit of 5% or so of the total) $10 trillion of goods and services each year. Africa could produce and consume a lot more without America producing and consuming one jot less. It so happens that the case for more aid, provided of course that it is well spent, is strong-but the industrialised countries do not need to become any less rich before Africa can become a lot less poor. The wealth of the wealthy is not part of the problem. To believe otherwise, however, is very much part of the problem.

When someone complains that the US uses a disproportionate amount of resources, or the rich are "too rich", they are making a foolish argument. A world without America would not be more equitable, except in the sense that everyone in it would be substantially poorer than they are.

And indeed, as trade has liberalized, and the economy increasingly globalized, the poor have been getting richer all over the world. Life expectancy has been constantly increasing and infant mortality declining in the developing world for the last 50 years. These are the two most-widely accepted measures of general well-being, and they show constant improvements in the lives of even the most impoverished inhabitants of the earth.

The redistributionists are troubled by the thought that rich people run the world. But, as P.J. O'Rourke points out[5], the alternative doesn't seem to be a lot better.

[T]he real alternative to the power of the rich is not the power of the poor but plain, simple power. If we don't want the world's wealth to be controlled by people with money then the alternative

---

5. "Closing the Wealth Gap", Speech at a June, 1997 Cato Foundation conference in Shanghai, China.

is to have the world's wealth controlled by people with guns. Governments have plenty of guns.

The theory of this is quite good. The robber puts down his pistol, picks up the ballot box and steals from rich people instead of from you. But the reality is different. Witness the track record of collectivism in this century: The holocaust, Stalin's purges, the suffering caused by the Great Leap Forward here.

Redistributionist thinking has consigned more people to death and starvation and totalitarian repression in the last century alone than any other idea in the history of human civilization. And still it continues. Scores, hundreds—perhaps thousands—of Africans die every day while the collectivists spout the same errors, and agitate for the same failed "solutions" they have for decades.

But, at least it makes them feel compassionate, which is, really, the important thing.

If African nations, or Asian nations, or Central American nations want to be wealthy, then they can be. All they have to do is limit the scope and size of government, deregulate their markets, and trade freely with the rest of the world. We've known this to be the answer for 150 years now, ever since the British government scrapped the mercantilist Corn Laws, and opened their borders up to trade after the Napoleonic wars.

In other words, stop giving so much power to the people with the guns.

RENT CONTROL

Santa Monica, California, often referred to as "The People's Republic of Santa Monica", loves rent control. Or rather, the politicians who run Santa Monica love it. The residents who have to live with it, not so much.

Rent control is like any other price control regulation, such as a minimum wage. By distorting the price mechanism, price controls impose restrictions on its ability to reflect reality. Prices are no longer set by the interaction of supply and demand, but they are fixed at an artificial level.

But, as we discussed in the first chapter, the whole purpose of price is to give us clear signals about what is happening in the real world. When those signals are distorted, the effects are generally negative.

When prices are set artificially low, it naturally increases the demand for housing. Think about it. If you see an ad that says, "3 Bed, 3 Bath Apartment, 1800 Sq ft. Rent Control, $288/mo", wouldn't you jump at it? For one thing, you'd no longer have to live with the hairy troll you call a "roommate". Why you could use one bedroom for a bedroom, one for an office, and another as an exercise room.

Nice.

But, everyone else in the city with a troglodyte roommate saw that add, too. They are just as interested in that apartment as you are. Too many people now want apartments to supply the demand. The result is a shortage.

Notice that the amount of housing compared to the number of people is unchanged. The only thing that has changed is that artificially manipulating the price of housing has increased demand beyond what the supply can fulfill.

Previously, you had to live with a roommate because the price—which properly reflected the relationship between supply and demand—rationed the amount of housing by preventing people from hoarding it.

And the shortage isn't going to get any better, because chances are that prospective landlords are going to look elsewhere to build housing.

Once a tenant moves into an apartment, the landlord is prevented from raising the rent until the tenant moves out. The tenant also knows that if he moves out, his next apartment will cost substantially more than the current one. So, the turnover in housing is greatly reduced, because tenants want to stay in their rent-controlled apartment.

For the landlord this means that, as the price of repairs, materials, management staff, security, and other costs of ownership rise, his revenues will be restricted to the current level. This makes owning a rental property increasingly unprofitable.

By making the rental business less profitable, rent control reduces the incentive to build more rentals. As the population increases, the shortage in housing will grow more acute. Instead of an artificial shortage due to the distortion of the price rationing mechanism, a real scarcity of housing will result.

Also, as the costs of ownership begins to rise, owners can no longer afford to keep the property maintained to as high a standard, so the quality of rent-controlled housing begins to deteriorate.

Then the law of unintended consequences starts to kick in. The purpose of rent control is to provide affordable housing for lower and middle-class renters. This generally means that luxury housing is not rent controlled. So, developers begin concentrating on building luxury rental units, where the price they charge can vary over time as the costs of ownership and management rise.

This creates a result that is precisely the opposite of that which the rent control advocates intended. Luxury housing becomes relatively cheaper and more abundant—though not cheap enough for poor and middle-class tenants to occupy—while rent controlled housing becomes scarce, and of increasingly lower quality.

This is the standard end result of price controls, whether for rent or for labor.

The idea behind it is fundamentally flawed. It is the notion that government can legislate away the reality that obtains in the real world about supply, demand, and prices. But government action doesn't repeal reality, and it is foolish to believe otherwise.

To believe in rent control, you have to believe that people do not respond to incentives, and that people will willingly pay for a thing something other than what it costs.

When thinking about rent control, or any other proposed policy, it is always a wise idea to ask, "And then what will happen?" Identify the incentives that a proposed policy will create. Then ask the question again and again. You might be surprised at how many initially attractive sounding policies will have actual results that will dismay you.

HEALTH CARE

Another hot-button issue is the question of what to do about health care. The last time a serious attempt at universal health care coverage was made was during the Clinton Administration. Despite months of work on it by the then First Lady, Senator Hillary Rodham Clinton (D-NY), the plan died a quick death in congress.

Health care takes up 13% of our GDP. In fact, we spend more than most other industrialized countries. HealthPolicyMonitor.org, an international health policy reform network, reports that spending on health care in most industrialized countries, as a percentage of GDP, is substantially lower than ours.

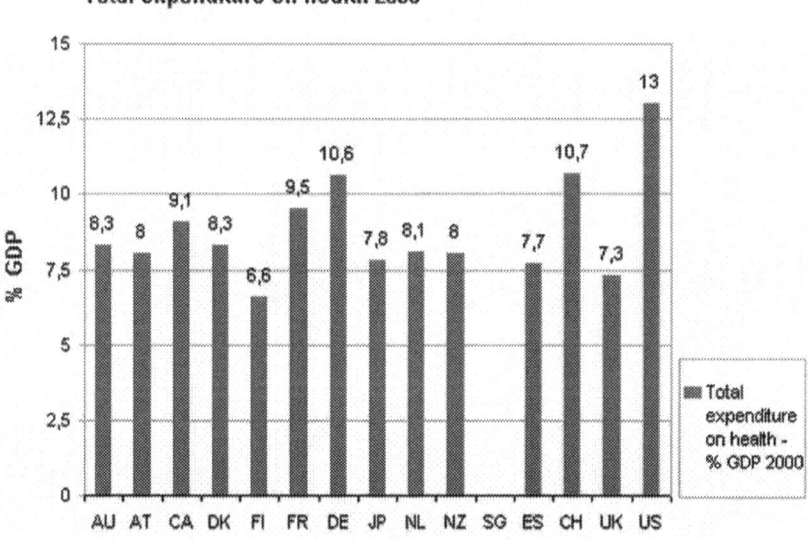

Figure 3: Health Care Spending as a Percentage of GDP in Indutrialized Nations

Most countries spend only 7%–9% on health care, compared to the 13% we spend in the US. Taken as a per-capita measure, the picture looks much the same.

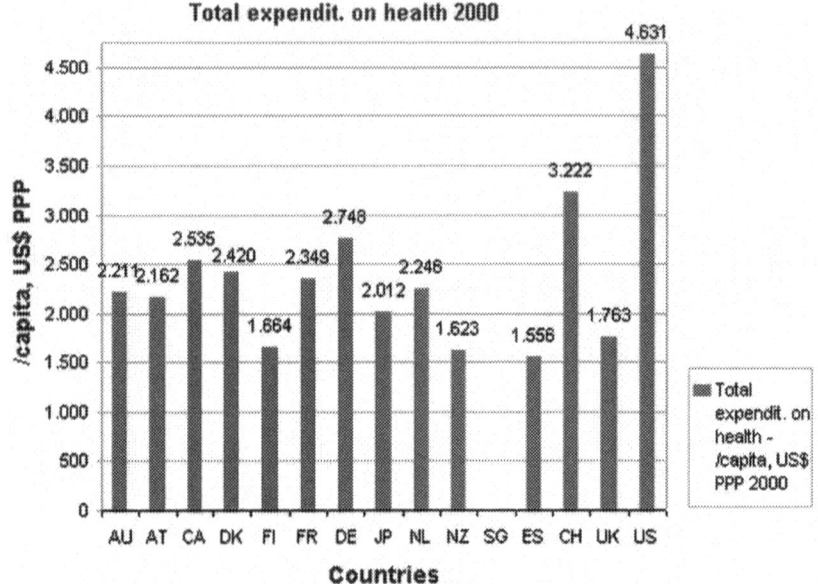

Figure 4: Per-Capita Health Care Spending in Industrialized Nations

Why is spending so much higher in the US, with its supposedly free-market system? Why is it, with all that spending, that regular medical coverage doesn't exist for 40 million Americans, when, in the rest of the industrialized world, there is 100% health coverage?

Something is deeply wrong with the financing of the US health-care system.

Part of the problem is that we really don't *have* a free market in health care. Individuals, by and large, don't buy health care policies. Health insurance is employer-provided. In effect, however, this is underwritten by the US government by making health care premiums deductible for businesses, which results in billions of dollars in lost tax revenues. And then, of course, you have to throw in the $300 billion or so that the state and federal governments spend outright to provide health care. And, of course, once you hit 65, you're on the government's health care gravy train, because you've got your Medicare, which also covers prescription drugs, now.

Why do we spend too much for health care in the US? The Heartland Institute, a public policy think-tank, has listed several reasons:

1) Government subsidies to health care increases demand by artificially lowering costs.

2) Favorable tax treatment of employer-provided health care has the same effect.

3) Lower-income people without health care must rely on emergency room health care delivery at substantially higher cost.

4) Health care buyers and sellers meet in a "market" that is heavily regulated by the government.

5) State governments increase health care costs by mandating benefit coverages.

6) State governments artificially reduce the supply of health care by requiring Certificates of Need before health care providers can expand services.

7) States interfere with the creation and operation of PPOs by fixing prices or the range of services they can offer.

So, really, we have what is, in many ways, the worst of both worlds. We have a market-based system, but one in which market incentives are minimized through regulation and subsidies. In effect, government policy bids up health care prices, while at the same time interfering with the market forces that keep a lid on prices.

It's no wonder that more and more people are looking at single-payer, government-provided health care as an alternative to what we already have. At the very least, a single payer system would end the inefficient and fragmented ways by which health care is currently purchased.

This is not a situation we can afford to ignore for long. The increasing expense of health care is becoming a key issue in, among other things, labor disputes.

For several months in 2003–2004, residents of Southern California were inconvenienced for months by two separate labor union strikes. A strike by the mechanics of Los Angeles' Metropolitan Transit Authority (MTA) left half a million commuters scrambling to find alternate means of transportation in LA County. Another strike, this time by the United Food and Commercial Workers Union (UFCW), affected the three main supermarket chains everywhere in the southern half of the state. Picket lines and empty shelves forced consumers to shop elsewhere—and often at higher prices—for their groceries.

In both cases, one of the central issues was the attempt by management to require employees to pay for a larger share of their health insurance coverage. In addition to asking for higher monthly contributions from the employees, employees were also asked to pay higher co-payments to cover a greater share of their medical costs.

The UFCW derided these proposals as simple corporate greed. The actual situation, however, was a little more complex than that. As management officials for both the supermarkets and the MTA pointed out, spiraling health care costs are making it increasingly difficult to provide health benefits to employees.

It is often said that, as California goes, so goes the nation. If so, then those events in California serve to remind us that health care is a problem that should—and inevitably will—concern us all.

For the last four years, the cost of health care and health insurance has risen by 11%–14% per year. At the time of this writing, it's expected to rise another 12% nationwide. In California, the California Healthcare Foundation estimates costs will rise by 14.7% over the current year (2004). Over the past three years, many businesses have seen the cost of health coverage increase by 50%.

The picture is just as disturbing for people who try to buy individual health care. The cost of an HMO plan from the non-profit Blue Shield of California costs over $300 per month, with a $500 deductible. For a family, the cost is much greater. If you have 1 spouse between 35 and 39, one spouse between 30 and 34, and two+ children, the costs for the

Blue Shield Spectrum PPO Plan 500 ($500 deductible) is $678 per month. Paying costs like that require either a very healthy amount of disposable income, or significant sacrifices. With costs like these, it's no wonder that 43 million Americans don't have health insurance.

Nor is it any wonder that, according to a 20 October, 2003, ABC News/Washington Post poll, 62% of Americans want some form of universal health care coverage and 78% of the respondents were dissatisfied with the cost of the nation's health care system. In fact, a majority was dissatisfied with the overall quality of the country's health care system. Clearly, a system where costs are doubling every seven or eight years, and where 54% of the customers are dissatisfied, is ripe for change. But, what sort of change?

In the short-term, a high priority must be given to restraining the rise in health care costs. One of the prime reasons for the increasing cost of health care is the cost of litigation. Medical liability costs are skyrocketing, and malpractice insurance for a physician costs up to $250,000 a year, now. Many doctors are simply dropping out of medicine, because their malpractice premiums are killing them. And who can blame them?

The only way to stop this expensive legal juggernaut is through tort reform. We must take a serious look at eliminating contingency fees and forcing lawyers to work strictly on an hourly basis, implementing some sort of "loser pays" tort system, or some combination of the two.

We must also look at ways to reduce health care demand. One way of doing this would be through the increased use of Medical Savings Accounts (MSAs). At the beginning of every calendar or fiscal year, the employer puts $2000–$3000 into an MSA for each employee. On top of that, the company buys a major medical policy for catastrophic health care problems. These types of policies are much less costly than traditional medical plans.

Any time the employee or his family needs to go to the doctor, the employee pays for it out of the MSA. At the end of the year, any money remaining in the MSA is either rolled over into the employee's

401(k)/IRA retirement plan, or the employee can take it as income after paying income taxes on it. Medical costs over and above the amount in the MSA would be covered by the major medical policy provided by the employer.

This would provide both primary and major medical care coverage to the employee, while at the same time reducing health care demand by providing an incentive for the employee to use as little of the MSA money as possible. The less the employee uses, the more money he gets at the end of the year. In essence, the MSA provides an incentive for the employee to ration his own health care.

Beyond cost-cutting measures such as these, however, the issue of universal health coverage must still be addressed.

One view is that some sort of single-payer national health system should be devised. Advocates of this kind of system point to Canada, where it has operated for years. Critics respond that such a system results in terribly high levels of taxation in order to fund it, and widespread rationing of health care in order to restrain costs.

But for many Americans, the idea of universal coverage remains a compelling one. Many people fear losing health care benefits for their families if they are laid off. The self-employed find it difficult to afford individual health plans. And people with employer-provided health benefits are seeing those benefits shrink or their costs rise—or both.

In such an environment, free-market critics of single-payer coverage must remind the public about the true nature and costs inherent in a single payer-system. The public should be reminded that, as American Medical Association president, Dr. Donald J. Palmisano, has said, "By implementing a single-payer system, the United States would be trading one problem for another."

In truth, the performance of single-payer health care has never been very encouraging. Such systems inevitably distort the market by—of course—distorting the price mechanism.

Single-payer health care systems are usually paid for by some form of progressive taxation. Doctors and other health care professionals are paid by the state, and patients do not pay any fees for services.

This works much like any other price control mechanism does, in that it increases demand for services, because the price each individual pays doesn't accurately reflect the actual cost of care. Because the payment comes out of taxes, the patient perceives visits to the doctor as "free". So, they go to the doctor more often, and for more minor complaints. There is no incentive for them to ration their own health care, so they don't.

Naturally, this stretches the available resources of the health care system, as doctors become health care providers of first resort.

After all, why take one of grandma's nasty home remedies for a minor problem when the doctor can give you real drugs? The word on the street is that if you drink enough of that prescription Robitussin, you can see God.

This increased demand increases the real cost of health care, even though the cost is hidden from the patient. Because the rationing function of prices is not allowed to work, other forms of rationing have to be implemented. This rationing usually takes the form of long waiting lists, even for quite serious medical conditions. Patients in Canada, for example, are forced to wait up to eight months for heart bypass operations.

This type of rationing can have serious health consequences, and increases the risk of death for such patients as they wait for life-saving medical procedures. The waiting lines for minor, elective procedures, such as vasectomies, are even longer.

And trying to get a cosmetic procedure like a face-lift or a tummy tuck is an exercise in futility.

Some countries attempt to reduce this problem by having a two track system where the public is allowed to purchase private health insurance, although they still must pay the national health tax. This really is a two-tier system, where those wealthy enough to afford it can bypass the public health system entirely, and get the best available health care on demand.

In countries like Canada, however, where private health insurance is banned, even that option is unavailable. Canadians, however, since the vast majority of them live within 100 miles of the US border, can and do travel to the United States to obtain health care, despite the higher cost.

If your "free" and universal health care system is forcing a significant number of citizens to obtain health care in a foreign country, then you probably haven't built a very good system.

And, by a number of indicators, the Canadians haven't. Most US hospitals have access to far more advanced medical treatments and technologies than do Canadian ones. For example, there are more Magnetic Resonance Imaging machines in Los Angeles than in the entire nation of Canada.

Implementing health care reform in the US is subject about which we need to think long and hard, but the move to a single-payer system such as Canada's is not the easy solution it seems.

WRAPPING IT UP

These are just a few of the major political economic issues that we face. And, in each case, the easy "compassionate" solutions are not precisely what they seem.

Of course, we feel sympathy for our fellow citizens who don't seem to be "making it". We are naturally attracted to policies that advocates assure us are humane and compassionate.

But the true measure of success in public policy is not how sincerely the advocates call for it, or how much concern they feel for the poor, or the uninsured. The only true measure of success is whether the policy actually solves the problem it was intended to solve.

This requires us to do a hard thing as voters and citizens. We can't simply settle for the policy that makes us feel better. We must each ask,

"What are the incentives such a policy will create? What are the unintended consequences of the policy?" In short, before we agree to a policy, we must ask, "And then, what will happen?"

It is harder to do this. And it may not be as emotionally satisfying to take a hard-eyed look at the advocates of compassion, and grill them about their proposals.

But it is an act of moral vanity to impose policies on the country that make us feel better about ourselves, while doing nothing to help the people they are supposed to help.

In this book, I have tried to give you some of the tools to ask probing, skeptical questions, and to view questions of policy from an economic point of view.

At the end of the day, however, all I can do is open the toolbox and show you the tools. How you use them...well, that's up to you.

Index

0-595-31699-9